D0221402

CREATING THE RESILIENT ORGANIZATION

A RapidResponse Management Program

DISCARDED

EDWARD DEEVY

PRENTICE HALL
Englewood Cliffs, New Jersey 07632

Prentice Hall International (UK) Limited, *London*
Prentice Hall of Australia Pty. Limited, *Sydney*
Prentice Hall Canada, Inc., *Toronto*
Prentice Hall Hispanoamericana, S.A., *Mexico*
Prentice Hall of India Private Limited, *New Delhi*
Prentice Hall of Japan, Inc., *Tokyo*
Simon & Schuster Asia Pte. Ltd., *Singapore*
Editora Prentice Hall do Brasil, Ltda., *Rio de Janeiro*

10 9 8 7 6 5 4 3 2

Library of Congress Cataloging-in-Publication Data

Deevy, Edward
   Creating the resilient organization : a rapid response
management program / Edward Deevy
      p.   cm.
   Includes index.
   ISBN 0-13-169624-6
   1. Organizational change--Management. 2. Organizational
effectiveness. I. Title.
HD58.D433 1995
658.4'06--dc20   95-10494
                                                       CIP

ISBN 0-13-169624-6

Prentice Hall
Career & Personal Development
Englewood Cliffs, NJ 07632

Simon & Schuster, A Paramount Communications Company

Printed in the United States of America

This book is dedicated to the memory of my brother, Andy. An accident in his early years threatened to leave him wheelchair-bound. He defied medical odds and went on to make valuable contributions as husband, parent and citizen. His resiliency in the face of the unexpected was a source of special inspiration.

ACKNOWLEDGMENTS

Significant contributions from colleagues, clients, friends and family have made this book possible. It would be impossible to list here everyone who has helped.

Kathleen Gilligan ("Kate") was my partner in developing the concept of RapidResponse management. My understanding of the need for mature work organizations to develop a high degree of resiliency grew out of our work together for client companies throughout the United States and in Europe.

Many valuable insights in this book can be traced to my work and the work of our consulting group, Deevy Gilligan International, with client organizations. Communication and dialogue with these clients has deepened my understanding of what it takes to transform established companies and institutions. For reasons of confidentiality the names of these individuals and their companies are not listed here. I thank them for enabling me to write a book that is grounded in reality.

My perspective on work organizations has been broadened by the experience of working with a variety of companies and institutions in Ireland and the UK. A colleague in Dublin, Denis McGrath, coordinated my work with schools, colleges and governmental agencies. Through a partnership with General Controls and Automation Ltd (GCAL) in Dun Laoghaire, Co. Dublin, I was able to work with executives and managers from leading business and industrial organizations. Jean Roberts of GCAL has been instrumental in maintaining the flow of transatlantic communications.

The list of people to whom I owe an intellectual debt is a long one. One group in particular has been a source of rich inspiration. Several years ago Kim Slack invited a few fellow members of the Greater Boston Organizational Development Network to join him in forming a reading group. Our monthly meetings have gone beyond reviewing books to a sharing of experiences and insights. I want to express appreciation to the regular members of our group: Cynthia Ingols, Kim Slack, Ken Farbstein, Martha Mueller, Tom Matera, Marilyn Darling, Tony DiBella, and Michelle Rapp.

A number of writers have contributed to my understanding of organizational transformation. The short list includes Peter Block, Meg Wheatley, Marvin Weisbord, Edgar Schein, Max DePree, Noel Tichy, Warren Bennis and Jack Stack.

The first draft of the manuscript was reviewed by several friends and colleagues. Valuable feedback was provided by George Dowd, Gerry Felski, Norah Lusignon, Leo Lusignon, Dan Tobin, Peggy MacInnis and Ken West. A colleague, Marcia Yudkin, provided useful insights on the publishing industry.

I acknowledge in a very special way the support and assistance of Kate Phillips. Kate edited various drafts of the manuscript and offered numerous suggestions. More than any other person, she has helped maKe this a book that is enjoyable to read. Thank you, Kate!

The production of this book is the result of what was truly a team effort. My agent, Mike Snell, delivered on his promise to "find a good home" for the manuscript. I want to acknowledge Tom Power, a senior editor at Prentice Hall, for constant support and for offering many helpful suggestions. I thank everyone at Prentice Hall involved

in bringing the book to the marketplace, including in particular Lauren Mazzola and Christine McCafferty for their promotional efforts.

Several friends helped sustain my energy throughout this project. Jack Caldwell, Diane Caldwell and Joan Glynn joined in celebrating important milestones. Likewise, my friends at Pedro Diego's were part of the support team. Steve Shea, with infectious enthusiasm, kept pointing to the opportunities for making a major contribution to work organizations that were in need of help. My friend, Mike Elmhirst, offered an occasional reminder on the importance of keeping the batteries charged with positive energy.

I am blessed to have a family that always supports my efforts, including the publication of this book. The extended family in the United States, including the Walshes and the Coulsons, provided encouragement and invaluable feedback. My London-based brother, Tom, provided a retreat to write the first draft of the manuscript. And Lena Deevy, despite her commitments as director of a social center in Boston, found time to support this project from beginning to end. My thanks to Lena and everyone who supported me along the way.

CONTENTS

FOREWORD

"All we have to show for three years of struggling is a stack of dust-covered manuals," one executive recently told me in reference to his company's aborted effort to effect meaningful change. His weary comment expresses a frustration shared by numerous managers and disillusioned workers over failed attempts to bring about a transformation of their organizations. These managers and workers have come to understand that "quick fix" initiatives, often involving high-priced consultants, really do little more than tinker at the edges of real problems.

The various improvement programs of the past decade, including total quality management and business process reengineering, have failed because they fail to address the core processes involved in transforming yesterday's bureaucratic organization into tomorrow's responsive enterprise. This book, the result of my own passionate conviction about the need for fundamental changes in the way traditional businesses are managed, evolved out of one crucial question: How do we *convince* executives and managers that they must do more than simply embrace the latest management fad? My belief is that organizational leaders will have the courage to make revolutionary changes when and only when they understand that such changes are an *indispensable* condition for competitiveness in the future.

In this book I make the case for a radical transformation of older companies and institutions by answering three basic questions:

- What is it about traditional work organizations that limits their ability to be competitive in a fast-paced business environment?
- What cultural or systemic changes must be made in order to regain competitiveness?
- How can we most effectively transform older bureaucracies into responsive high-performing enterprises?

This book directly challenges basic assumptions about what it takes to increase the competitiveness of older bureaucratic enterprises. At the heart of my argument is the view that the organization is a living system capable of self-organization and self-renewal—if the right conditions are created. This view is radically different from the "mechanical" view that underlies total quality management, business process reengineering, and other improvement efforts.

TWO UNIFYING THEMES

The basic assumption in this book is that, in the future, companies and institutions will need to be managed according to a fundamentally different set of management principles. This new approach is referred to as *RapidResponse management*. The goal is the creation of an organization that is flexible, agile, responsive, and capable of surviving and thriving in a turbulent environment. Throughout this book I describe the process of introducing RapidResponse management into traditional bureaucratic organizations.

We view RapidResponse Management as the foundation for building organizations that can cope with the turbulence and unpredictability of the modern business environment. This leads to the second theme throughout this book, namely, the need to create *resilient organizations*. The ultimate test for work organizations today can be summarized in one question: Are they sufficiently *resilient* to cope with an increasingly turbulent and unpredictable environment? *The basic ingredient of a resilient organization is a committed work force that is free to give the maximum effort.* The challenge is to unleash human energy. Companies and institutions must develop within themselves the capacity for continual self-renewal. This book provides the information needed for turning your company or institution into a *resilient* organization. RapidResponse management principles and practices are the basis for building tomorrow's resilient organization.

With the end of the Cold War and the impending millennium the attention of political leaders is now directed to the profound transformation taking place in society. Vice President Al Gore has been a highly visible spokesman for the need to "reinvent government." Speaker of the House Newt Gingrich wants to move Congress into the Information Age. Gingrich draws his inspiration from Alvin and Heidi Toffler, a Chicago-based couple who have reemerged as America's leading futurists. The Tofflers believe that the world is in the throes of a transition to the "third wave," a revolution in information technology and rapid change that follows the first two waves, the agricultural revolution and the industrial revolution.

Gore and Ginrich are not the only leaders calling for transformation. Robert Reich was advocating a revolution in management practices long before he became Secretary of Labor. Texas billionaire, Ross Perot, has focused attention on the need to have productive companies as the foundation of our economy.

This book speaks directly to the agendas of Gore, Gingrich, Reich, and Perot. These leaders all understand that revolutionary changes are needed. Our Industrial Age organizations - and we have hundreds of thousands of them - will need to undergo profound changes in management practices if they are to make it into the Information Age. This book provides a bold blue-print for those executives and managers who are willing to move forward.

WHO SHOULD READ THIS BOOK

In a broad sense, I wrote this book for all people who understand at a visceral level that the old answers and mechanistic formulas are not working. Specifically, this book is written for five groups of people:

1. Organization leaders who want to create an entrepreneurial work environment
2. Both internal and external consultants who are responsible for guiding transformation efforts
3. People in the public arena who see themselves as having a role in creating a more productive and competitive economy
4. Academics and students who need a real-life perspective on organizational change theory
5. The layperson who wants to better understand the revolution taking place in the workplace

This will be of primary interest to those leaders who each day face the challenge of making their organizations more responsive to a fast-changing marketplace. During the past ten years, as a change management consultant, I have met many executives who understand the need to make fundamental changes in management practices, but who underestimate the complexity of this task. These managers assume, somewhat naively, that a mature organization can be transformed by following a step-by-step formula. This "mechanical fix" attitude is reinforced by "vendors" who sell prepackaged programs for improving organizational performance. Because many business leaders simply don't want to admit that culture change is difficult, management gurus who offer easy fixes can always find a receptive audience. However, the manager looking for a quick and simple fix resembles the individual who goes to a psychotherapist and says, "I have lost my job and my marriage is in serious trouble— give me the formula for getting my life back on track!" This book is for managers who understand that changing deeply ingrained attitudes and behaviors is not a simple task.

While it is possible to draw a diagram illustrating the steps of the change process, in real life change cannot be implemented according to a precise step-by-step formula. In this book, therefore, I provide the broad framework for understanding the dynamics of organizational change in language that is comprehensible. It is my hope that visionary business leaders who are committed to leading their businesses into the future will find in this book a map to guide their journey.

HOW THIS BOOK IS ORGANIZED

Following the example of good murder mysteries, I have introduced the reader to the critical facts in Chapter One. Consider this a "must read" chapter, the key to understanding everything that follows. It presents the conceptual framework for building a high-performance work organization and introduces the reader to the three "secrets" of RapidResponse management.

The unifying theme throughout this book is the need for older, established organizations to undergo a transformation if they are to successfully compete in an increasingly turbulent environment. The rationale for radically changing the culture of older companies and institutions is spelled out in Chapter Two and Chapter Three. Each one of three conditions for creating a RapidResponse work organization is described in Chapters Four, Five, and Six. The remaining chapters are designed to answer the question: How do we transform the culture of an older organization? Among the critical issues addressed are the following:

Why *vision* can be a motivating force for change (Chapter Seven)

The need for trustworthy leaders (Chapter Eight)

How to get middle management to buy in (Chapter Nine)

A strategy for quickly changing the whole organization (Chapter Ten)

The psychology of *resistance* (Chapters Eleven and Twelve)

How to identify *resilient* employees (Chapter Thirteen)

Chapter Fourteen explores the challenge of maintaining a high level of responsiveness to the marketplace, and Chapter Fifteen provides the rationale for maintaining balance between work and life. Chapter Sixteen illustrates some of the broader applications of the RapidResponse paradigm, and Chapter Seventeen revisits the basics for building the entrepreneurial enterprise.

A WORD ABOUT THE DESIGN OF THIS BOOK

Interspersed throughout the text of the book are sidebars with anecdotes, minicase studies, practical guidelines, and selected quotations. You will also see highlighted key sentences from the text. The highlighted text makes quick review possible. The sidebars serve to illustrate the text with practical how-to information. There is a short summary paragraph at the end of each chapter highlighting the key idea presented. The busy reader can use these summaries to identify the chapters that are of the most interest.

A CALL TO ACTION

This volume sets forth an optimistic vision of the workplace where both people and profits can flourish. The aim is to inspire people to action, as well as to inform. You will find in this book everything you need to know about introducing RapidResponse management. Because each work organization has its own unique personality, the three core concepts must be adapted to each situation; the idea is not to create RapidResponse clones but to address the idiosyncratic needs of each business organization.

Recently, a growing number of consultants have begun to place major emphasis on changing the "architecture" of the organization, arguing that "function follows form." What they overlook is the fact that all the structural redesign in the world will not bring about real organizational transformation unless the people in the organization undergo an internal change. An organization is a collection of people, and these individuals must experience change at the emotional as well as the intellectual level. This book is an appeal to readers to reconsider their most deeply held assumptions about how the workplace is organized and managed.

In closing, I invite you to share my vision of an organization where all employees have an ownership stake and are able to contribute without the oppressive constraints of bureaucracy. Older work organizations do not have to die or fade away. They can be transformed into responsive and resilient high-performing enterprises for the twenty-first century.

North Andover, Massachusetts   Edward Deevy
May, 1995

C H A P T E R   1

BEYOND ORDER AND STABILITY:
Leading in a Turbulent Environment

I was compelled to begin work on this book several years ago when I received a request from a group of health care executives to present a talk on "Managing in a Turbulent Environment." In reflecting on this assignment, I found myself going back to an experience I'd had as a manager over 20 years before. In the late 1960s, I was director of a Vista project in the Deep South. My job was to provide focus and direction for the 20 to 25 young professionals who were engaged in offering technical assistance to indigenous community groups. Our challenge was to respond quickly to emerging needs in a highly dynamic environment. The Vista group, despite the diversity of its members and a free-wheeling style of operation, acquired a strong reputation for having the ability to adapt to sudden and unexpected developments in the community.

My primary concern, as a resource to members of the Vista project, was to minimize bureaucratic constraints and to support team members in their various endeavors. However, the federal government, like other large bureaucracies, worked to ensure that operations

1

were in strict control and that policies and procedures were being followed. In line with this desire for order and predictability, government administrators requested that a detailed plan of future activities be developed, using the management by objectives (MBO) planning process. MBO is a step-by-step methodology for planning how organizational resources will be used over a three- to five-year period. The process begins with a statement of goals and objectives. The time-phased objectives are broken down into a series of specific activities that are sequenced in such a way as to make achievement of the overall goals possible. Not surprisingly, given the dynamic nature of the environment in which they operated, members of the group were not inclined to expend energy on a detailed planning process. They were more interested in increasing the responsiveness of the group to emerging issues than in developing hypothetical scenarios for the future. Clearly, the MBO planning process presupposed an environment that was stable and predictable. At an intuitive level, I understood that traditional management practices, with their emphasis on order and predictability, were of limited value in a situation where a quick response was desirable.

The government's request for an MBO planning document induced our whole group to spend a weekend at a retreat facility exploring opportunities and possibilities for future action. Among the questions addressed: What are the external trends that will impact our future activities? What are project strengths and weaknesses when it comes to responding to emerging issues? What is the future we want to create? The process engaged in over the weekend developed into something now referred to as *future search*. Members of the group returned from the retreat energized and with a renewed sense of purpose.

Back at our headquarters, I was given the task of translating the ideas generated by the group into MBO format. Adapting visionary ideas to an outdated strategic planning model demanded a considerable amount of creativity.

My experience of managing the Vista project highlighted for me two contrasting views of work organizations: a "bureaucratic" model that assumed management *had the power to make the organization behave in a certain manner* and the "living system" model that assumed work organizations *had the natural capacity to operate as self-organizing and self-renewing entities.* The "bureaucratic" view, with its emphasis on a "scientific" approach to performance issues, would dominate management thinking during the following decades and into the 1990s.

ORGANIZATIONS IN TROUBLE:
THE *ENGINEERING* SOLUTION

Let me fast-forward from managing in a turbulent social environment in the 1960s to the unstable *business environment* of the mid-1980s. In the intervening years, I had held a succession of management positions, had obtained a doctorate in organizational psychology, and had taught management courses at a large university. Now I found myself consulting with older established companies and institutions in the United States and Europe as they sought to adapt to radical changes taking place in the marketplace. Two decades of workplace experience led me to conclude that bureaucracies could only develop the responsiveness demanded by the marketplace if they underwent a *cultural transformation.*

To meet these needs, my consulting group, Deevy Gilligan International, focused primarily on changing the mind-set of employees and on reducing bureaucracy to create responsive market-focused enterprises. Our catchwords were *process, relationships, self-organizing systems,* and *energy flow.* The larger business community, however, was not ready to embrace the concepts behind these words. Management persisted in thinking of work organizations as mechanical entities that could somehow be "fixed."

By the mid-1980s, the quality movement, with its emphasis on statistical tools and techniques, was picking up momentum. This movement was to become a powerful bandwagon acquiring the status of "true religion" among consultants and managers.

The first introduction of Japanese management in the early 1980s was in the form of *quality circles.* This technology, introduced in response to a decline in America's manufacturing competitiveness, did little to change traditional management practices. Quality circles became a mere appendage to existing hierarchical structures, and thus results were short lived. A more comprehensive version of Japanese management was introduced under the name *total quality management (TQM)*. This amalgam of practices, including a variety of tools and techniques that had been used in the past, was presented as a panacea for every kind of organization from manufacturing plant to hospital to government agency.

Like their predecessors who offered MBO as the scientific way to manage a company, the proponents of TQM believed an analytic approach, based on hard data, was the key to improved organizational performance. However, TQM and its derivative, *business process reengineering*, are based on a mechanical view of organizations that sees improvement of the "parts" as leading to transformation of the whole. This same mechanical view had inspired Frederick Taylor— remembered for his efforts in the 1920s to improve organizational performance through "scientific management." Indeed, an *engineering* mentality has dominated attempts to improve or redesign work organizations from Taylor to Michael Hammer, the modern guru of process reengineering.

THE "FIX" THAT DIDN'T WORK

We now know that over 75% of all TQM and business process reengineering efforts fail to deliver on their promises. In a 1992 article, I set forth some of the key reasons for this lack of success. The failure of these mechanistic approaches pointed to the need for a new view of what organizations really are and how they can be changed. It became increasingly clear that traditional bureaucratic organizations, designed for a stable and predictable environment, were ill-equipped to respond to a highly dynamic and constantly evolving marketplace. Reengineering and TQM represented efforts to repair an organizational entity that was inherently incapable of coping with instability and turbulence.

My understanding of organizational dynamics has evolved over several decades. Childhood experiences on the family farm had shown me that even very challenging goals could be accomplished through natural, nonbureaucratic work processes. Early study of philosophy, including the work of Tielhard de Chardin, reinforced a belief in the ability of individuals and groups to evolve to higher levels of consciousness. The experience of directing a Vista project had led me to consider the possibility of work organizations as self-organizing systems with the capacity for continuous self-renewal. In consulting work with hospitals, manufacturing plants, schools, and a variety of other organizations, I found myself paying close attention to the invisible forces that were at work.

Before long, it became clear to me that large investments in programs and consultants often did not result in the necessary changes. In one large utility company, we found that after a $1 million investment in TQM, the company had built up an elaborate bureaucracy consisting of trainers, facilitators, and over 70 quality improvement teams. However, all this effort, with its cumbersome support infrastructure, had no appreciable impact on the ability of this company to respond to changes in the marketplace. We observed this phenomenon in a variety of organizations, including one 300-bed acute care community hospital. The hospital was typical in that TQM was introduced with high expectations and considerable hype, but within two years, it was getting bogged down under the weight of its own bureaucracy. Management came to the realization that all the training sessions and team meetings had made little impact on the ability of the hospital to respond effectively to a turbulent health care marketplace.

It needs to be acknowledged that the tools and techniques of total quality management and business reengineering, if properly used, *can be highly effective in improving specific work processes.* However, despite the scientific aura associated with these technologies, they are not effective in bringing about a transformation of the *whole* organization. As I will suggest later, there is a role for TQM and reengineering in the streamlining and debureaucratizing of older companies and institutions, but that role is a limited one.

A NEW REQUIREMENT:
SPEED, RESPONSIVENESS, AND RESILIENCY

Doing business in today's unstable business environment requires a deep understanding of the inner dynamics of work organizations. The old paradigm of an organization as a mechanical entity that can be "fixed" when broken is inadequate. *The challenge for organizations today is to develop a new organizational form, one with the capability for continuously responding to change.*

This need for responsiveness is not confined to the business sector. Several years ago, the U.S. Army created a rapid deployment force, operating outside the normal constraints of military bureaucracy, that could respond to sudden and unexpected disturbances around the world. During the 1992 presidential election, the Clinton campaign staff created a rapid response capability at headquarters in Little Rock, Arkansas. Recently we have seen attempts to create a rapid response capability in a wide variety of organizations, including public sector agencies. In Massachusetts, for example, the Registry of Motor Vehicles established walk-in "license express" offices in shopping malls as part of an overall strategy of making the Registry a rapid response organization.

The business community is beginning to consider a new paradigm of the work organization as a self-renewing system that has the potential to be highly responsive to the environment. The proponents of this new view include Meg Wheatley, author of *Leadership and the New Science* (San Francisco: Berrett-Koehler, 1992). Wheatley believes that insights gained from new science have opened the door to a deeper understanding of human systems.

Several years ago my partner, Kathleen Gilligan, and I coined the word *RapidResponse* as shorthand to describe a new organizational entity. We had in mind an organization that has the *resilience* and *versatility* to cope with changing environmental conditions. RapidResponse represents an alternative to the view of work organizations as bureaucratic, top-down structures—a view that has prevailed since the beginning of the nineteenth century. In the traditional bureaucratic organization, order, stability and a "scientific" approach to improvement were valued. Maintaining *control* and *order* was a prerequisite for success. The *RapidResponse* organization, on the other hand, is viewed as a living system that thrives on chaos and disequilibrium and that has a built-in ability to adapt to changes in the environment. As indicated in the foreword, *RapidResponse management* is the foundation on which to build tomorrow's *resilient organization.*

Defining the Future: *RapidResponse*

For several years at DGI, we searched for a word that would best describe the key ingredient for success in tomorrow's marketplace. We wanted to capture the notion of *responsiveness* to the marketplace. However, we understood that this responsiveness would need to be combined with nimbleness and agility. Our in-the-trenches research clearly indicated that it was the ability to respond *quickly* to the environment that would separate winners from losers.

To communicate the combination of quickness and responsiveness needed in the new business environment, we coined the word *RapidResponse*. We use *RapidResponse* to convey the fact that in the future there is no response *other than* rapid. A slow response, an inflexible response, a bureaucratic response, a "not-invented-here" response, a "we'll get to it tomorrow" response are all kisses of death for the organization of the future. The word *RapidResponse* describes the organization that is capable of continuously adapting to the needs of the marketplace. We sometimes refer to that new organizational entity as the *resilient organization.*

RAPIDRESPONSE MANAGEMENT: A NEW SET OF ASSUMPTIONS

How does the RapidResponse organization differ from the bureaucratic model? The short answer is to say that these two models differ in the *fundamentals*. In seminars and keynote speeches I highlight three key differences.

1. The RapidResponse organization is based on "commitment" rather than "control."

The assumption is that real motivation comes from *within* the individual. Rejected is the idea that management can somehow "drive" change. While many managers speak of "getting results through people," they seem mostly determined to "make things happen" through a variety of strategies and techniques. What is needed is a shift from the *control* paradigm to the *commitment* paradigm. A turbulent, uncertain environment demands that people have the freedom to respond without having to deal with bureaucratic constraints.

2. The RapidResponse organization is a self-organizing system that has the potential for continuous self-renewal.

Our evolving understanding of the work organization as a self-organizing, living system has been enhanced by deeper understandings of the universe derived from chaos theory and quantum physics. We know from the natural sciences that a self-organizing system has the capacity for renewal and growth. In contrast, a machine tends to wear down. Many of the improvement programs introduced in recent years were based on the "mechanical view" of organizations.

Bureaucracy, with its emphasis on maintaining control and order, is inherently antithetical to self-organization. In promoting bureaucratic equilibrium, management hides from the processes that foster life and change. Evidence from the world of nature suggests that stability will lead to atrophy, and indeed, traditional bureaucracies often seem to be following the second law of thermodynamics, the so-called "laziness" law. They survive in a state of inertia. In their worst form, these bureaucracies produce employees who look like characters from *The Night of the Living Dead*.

A distinctive feature of the self-organizing RapidResponse organization is resiliency rather than stability. Disequilibrium and the ability to cope with the unexpected is valued over order and predictability. Everything is open and susceptible to change.

Meg Wheatley, in discussing the new science, points out the inherent *orderliness* that can be found in self-organizing systems.

Order is a natural phenomenon that can be achieved without a preengineered design. All you need is a clear definition of what the organization is trying to do and how people should conduct themselves given the situation at hand. Indeed, the responsive organization of the future will have much less management than its bureaucratic predecessor. The RapidResponse organization is built around a set of core competencies that give it a sense of identity and the ability to relate with the environment.

The concept of the organization as a dynamic self-renewing entity is helpful in understanding why mechanistic approaches do not hold the key to building the high performance organization. While TQM and reengineering have value as tools for streamlining specific work processes, they are not capable of unleashing the energy that is at the core of a self-renewing system. These technologies fail to capitalize on the capacity of work organizations to self-organize and self-renew.

3. In a RapidResponse enterprise organizational form takes shape from the necessary relationships.

In a 1992 speech at the Irish Science and Technology Centre in Dublin, Ireland, I illustrated the shift from the bureaucratic organization to the Rapid Response organization by using Figure 1.1:

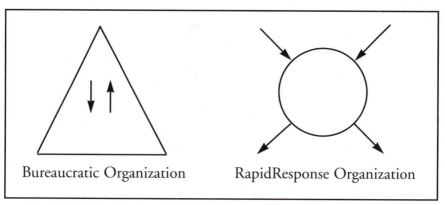

Bureaucratic Organization   RapidResponse Organization

Figure 1.1.
Two contrasting designs for work organizations.

The pyramid figure on the left illustrates the traditional hierarchical organization with its top-down management structure. It is a closed system with the energy flowing toward the top. The diagram on the right represents the interaction of the RapidResponse enterprise with its environment. Two arrows show an inflow of energy from the external environment and two arrows show energy flowing from the organization into the marketplace. I wanted to illustrate the continuous exchange of energy between the organization and the environment—an essential feature of a RapidResponse work organization.

I later discovered that my RapidResponse diagram was similar to the "S" (scattered) matrix used by scientists in symbolically representing the flow of energy between particles. It was an interesting coincidence, given the fact that I was trying to communicate the highly dynamic relationship between the organization and the environment. I wanted to suggest that the business organization of the future needs to have the capability of modifying its form to respond to a rapidly changing marketplace. The resilience and versatility of the RapidResponse organization and its ability to cope with turbulence comes from operating as a self-organizing entity, not from a bureaucratic structure. In the future there will be no "one-size-fits-all" structure for organizations.

Unlike the bureaucratic organization, illustrated in Figure 1.1 as a closed pyramid, the RapidResponse organization is an open system that draws energy and vitality from the environment. Responsiveness to the environment is a natural outcome of the organization as a living system. The form of the RapidResponse organization supports the relationships that are needed for the organization to fulfill its purpose. This form can change in response to internal or external demands. While traditional bureaucracies were designed for vertical communication, the RapidResponse model suggests a horizontal flow of activity from within the organization toward the external environment.

CREATING THE RAPIDRESPONSE WORKPLACE: THREE CONDITIONS

I have delineated key differences between the bureaucratic model of the work organization that has prevailed for over 150 years and a new way of thinking about organizations. Clearly, the RapidResponse model is not conceived of as an improvement on the old model but as a *fundamentally different* way of looking at how organizations function and how work gets done. The question arises: How do we transform a traditional bureaucracy into the new mode of operating? Before addressing this important question, we must consider the *magnitude* of the change that needs to be made.

There are times in human history when people are called upon to make a major shift in the way they view reality. A frequently cited example of a paradigm shift has to do with the shape of the world. For a long time the world had been viewed as flat. When, in the Middle Ages, Copernicus presented evidence to the contrary, people were forced to reconsider the old paradigm. This is an analogy for the kind of shift in thinking required as we reconsider the nature of work organizations. The old "command and control" model is now giving way to a new mental model derived from a deeper understanding of science, social psychology, and anthropology.

The word *transformation* is used to describe the shift from the old mode of operating to the new RapidResponse mode. What you are reading is a handbook on how to make this shift. Three core "conditions" for converting a traditionally managed organization into a resilient, self-organizing enterprise capable of continuously responding to the environment are identified. These conditions, taken together, help create an environment where entrepreneurial energy is unleashed. Each "condition" can be customized to the needs of the particular organization.

In later chapters I refer to these core conditions as the "Three Secrets of RapidResponse management." They are "secrets" in the sense that they are outside the traditional paradigm of how organizations are managed. As previously indicated, these three management principles are the basis for building tomorrow's *resilient organization*.

Condition 1. Allow each person to keep score.

It has been said that information is the solar energy of high performance organizations. A responsive organization has a high degree of consciousness about its purpose and its performance within the environment. Everyone has access to information on "the business of the business." What needs to be changed is how people at all levels relate to the enterprise; giving people "bits" of information is no substitute for treating people as *insiders* who have access to the "big picture." Mobilizing people to respond quickly to changes in the environment is extremely difficult when employees are operating in a vacuum. In the bureaucratic organization, information is the tool for exercising managerial control; in the RapidResponse organization, it is the fuel that transforms all activity.

How to create an organization where everyone "knows the score" will be explored in Chapter Three.

Condition 2. Create a free flow of activity in the direction of the customer.

As a young person growing up, I was intrigued by the meandering of a stream that flowed through the family farm. Despite the changing contours of the river banks the water always seemed to be moving relentlessly toward its destination. That river has become for me a metaphor for the free flow of energy and activity that characterizes a responsive work organization. An organization where the human energy stagnates and where bureaucratic structures or policies create obstacles to a free flow of activity is not likely to respond quickly to changes in the environment.

The experience of growing up on the family farm provided another useful metaphor. Each harvesting season we confronted the challenge of getting crops from the fields in constantly changing weather conditions. In retrospect, I view that experience as my first encounter with a self-organizing work group. Here I observed a natural flow of activity, with each family member contributing according to their potential and with everyone fully aware of changing conditions. The ability to respond quickly was clearly enhanced by the fact that there were no bureaucratic obstacles interfering with the free flow of activity.

The bureaucratic model has its roots in the early nineteenth century, when the business environment was stable and predictable. The elaborate infrastructure that evolved from that time reflected a need by management to exercise control. However, as I have already indicated, understandings derived from new science, including chaos theory, suggest that there is a natural order built into living systems. Quantum physics has increased our awareness of the interconnectedness that exists within a system. For too long we have artificially broken up the work of organizations into departments, functions and roles. We need to see the *whole* rather than the parts. Today's turbulent environment requires that we *debureaucratize* work organizations and allow energy to flow naturally across boundaries.

As we have noted, the tools and techniques of total quality management and business process reengineering have a role to play in redesigning and streamlining existing work processes. The late Dr. Edwards Deming was an outspoken advocate of *process simplification.* In later years he was critical of those consulting firms which created elaborate, prepackaged quality improvement programs.

In Chapter Four I will provide a six-step model that can be used in streamlining the flow of activity across organizational boundaries. The emphasis will be on simplicity at any cost.

Condition 3. Give each person a stake in the outcome.

The business of management consulting is becoming analogous to the fast-food industry, with various gurus competing with each other to come up with formulas that sound good. Much of what is written and said is for popular consumption. Missing is a real exploration of what it takes to *motivate* people. One casualty of "fast-food" consulting and simplistic approaches to performance improvement is the concept of *employee participation.* After Peters and Waterman wrote their book on "excellent" companies in 1982, the urge for instant change took over in corporate America. Suddenly, employees were wearing name tags proclaiming that they were "associates" or "partners." These changes were merely cosmetic, with the relationship between the employee and the enterprise remaining unchanged; indeed, the concept of participation was actually devalued. Even efforts to involve employees on quality improvement teams represented, in my opinion, little more than tokenism.

The RapidResponse organization is built on *genuine* involvement of people at all levels, not on the illusion of participation. The psychology is simple and obvious: *If people feel they have a real stake in the success of an enterprise they can be mobilized to help that business to respond to changes in the environment.* However, we need to go beyond giving people a psychological investment and make it possible for them to have a financial stake. Employees who see a direct connection between the success of the enterprise and their own economic welfare will have a strong incentive to work hard. I refer to this phenomenon as *enlightened self-interest.*

In Chapter Five I will identify the practical issues to be considered as companies develop innovative ways of sharing ownership with employees. My intention is not to offer a ready-made formula for compensating employees but to argue the case for ensuring employees have ownership in the enterprise.

TRANSFORMING THE *WHOLE* ORGANIZATION: A "BLITZ" STRATEGY

Can an organization, designed according to traditional bureaucratic assumptions, be converted into a self-organizing system that is capable of continuously adapting to an unstable and unpredictable environment? What process can be used to bring about this kind of transformation? These are questions that I have wrestled with for over 20 years. After Kathleen Gilligan and I formulated the concept of the RapidResponse organization, we developed a transformation strategy that could be implemented over a 2- to 4-year period. Known as the *DGI change model,* it included five sequential steps:

Step 1. An assessment of organizational culture.

Step 2: The gathering of leaders: a "visioning" session for top management held at an off-site location.

Step 3. Training sessions to help middle management move from the "control paradigm" to the "commitment paradigm."

Step 4. Large-group sessions to help rank-and-file employees acquire ownership for the vision.

Step 5. Follow-up.

In work with older companies I became increasingly frustrated with the pace of change. It seemed to take forever to get to step 4—the involvement of employees at-large. The questions I asked myself at this time went to the core of *how* change happens: Can we involve the experience and expertise of everyone in the organization? Can people create their own responses to change? A breakthrough came when I began to understand that involving the *whole* organization up-front would greatly accelerate the transformation process. I concluded that successful transformation had more to do with *who was in the room* than any other single variable. There was no point in management charging forward if the "troops" were still feeling like outsiders.

While the DGI change model was highly effective in getting management involved, I came to favor a process known as *future search* because of its potential to get the whole organization quickly involved. In my view, "future search" is a highly effective and efficient approach to moving an older established organization in the direction of becoming a self-organizing system. The new approach is faster because the whole system is involved within 3-6 months.

A future search conference involves all parts of the organization in looking at its future. Ordinarily, the conference will have 75 to 150 participants. In larger organizations a vertical slice of the organization is invited to attend. Each significant constituency is represented. Several sessions may be scheduled to involve a critical mass of employees. While there is no cook book formula for conducting a future search conference, the program usually lasts two to three days and is designed to allow participants to explore the past, the present and the future. It is a dynamic *process*, not a technique. The conference is managed by a team of two or three facilitators experienced in group and organizational dynamics. Customers may be invited to participate. Outside experts, if used, are given a very limited role.

In recent work I have referred to the future search conference as the "blitz method" to communicate its sudden and powerful impact on traditional bureaucratic work organizations. Unlike incremental top-down change strategies, this approach is designed to cause a quick, major shift in attitudes and behaviors throughout the organization. The potential for this kind of process to unleash energy was first brought home to me when I worked with the Vista project in the late 1960s. What impressed me at that time was the possibility that any group could create its own future by engaging everyone in the discussion of a few fundamental questions.

A widely reported Arthur D. Little survey of 300 senior executives found that only 18% of them felt that their recent major change efforts had yielded substantial results. Somehow, despite all the consultants and training sessions, the impact of most interventions appears to be minimal; the effort to transform organizations does not usually go deep enough. With future search, *everyone* has ownership for the decisions that are made. While this process can have a powerful impact on the organization, the momentum gained must be reinforced and sustained by follow-up activities.

As future search becomes more widely known and used throughout the United States and abroad, we have to hope that it will not be turned into another "mechanical fix." Those who use future search need to know that change is a capacity built into nature and that the challenge is to foster natural processes of growth and development. We need to stop trying to *change people* and realize that with the right *conditions*, change will naturally happen. What we must understand is that people have a need for access to more relationships, to work in an information-rich environment, and to truly understand why they are working together and what they are trying to accomplish. Future search is the ideal way to open up the organization to the new RapidResponse mode of operating.

In recent years our consulting group developed the *five-stage blitz change strategy* as a framework for getting the whole organization involved. The process of implementing the blitz strategy is described in Chapter Ten.

LETTING CHANGE HAPPEN

After almost three decades of working with organizations, including 15 years in various management and executive positions, I have come to understand the futility of trying to *make things happen* in organizations. The secret is to let the natural self-organizing dynamics take over. The role of management is to create the *conditions* for building a RapidResponse enterprise. There are a few basics that must be addressed by management as part of the transformation process. Information is the raw energy that fuels the process of self-renewal, and it should be available throughout the entire organization. Additionally, older, established companies need to undertake a process of debureaucratization. As already indicated, an organization can be responsive only if workers are free of unnecessary constraints. Finally, people need to have some real motivation to want to respond to the marketplace. Giving people a financial stake in the enterprise is one way to guarantee that entrepreneurial juices will flow.

Several years ago I attended a seminar in which the presenter used an overhead transparency to show the steps involved in "creating a TQM organization." The transparency showed a matrix with 24 boxes, each containing an activity that would need to be implemented. I was aghast at the notion that the complex task of changing an organization could be reduced to this prescribed matrix of activities. However, upon reflection, it quickly became clear that, for someone with the mechanical viewpoint, this matrix made sense. Alternatively, for someone viewing the organization as a living system with invisible forces, the matrix seemed absurd! This incident illustrates the two fundamentally different views of organizational reality that have been highlighted in this chapter.

In working with the Vista project in the late 1960s, I "discovered" that an organization can function well in an unstable environment if the members have a few guiding principles to serve as a frame of reference. One key lesson from that formative experience: *The less bureaucracy, the greater the ability to respond to unexpected circumstances.* The role of management is to create the right conditions for organizations to operate as self-organizing and self-renewing entities. Managers need to have faith that if they give up control, the result will not be chaos.

THE SEARCH MUST CONTINUE

The RapidResponse model presented here grew out of research and experience that has spanned three decades. The search for organizational forms better suited for the twenty-first century must continue.

We must continue to question our basic assumptions about what works and does not work. The bureaucratic model has become dysfunctional. The RapidResponse model offers a useful framework for older organizations as they seek to transform themselves. I believe we will see different models emerge as we move into the future. We need to stay open to new ideas and keep our eyes on the horizon.

Failures in "TQM" and "reengineering" force us to think about organizations differently. An underlying assumption throughout this book is that we need to learn how to change the way we foster change. We need to continue to rethink how organizations fundamentally are put together, what people need when they work inside organizations, and how managers can maximize the productivity and increase the rewards of organizational life. The goal must be the creation of work organizations that are constantly adaptive, versatile, and resilient and that people want to work in. We have to create the conditions that will allow organizations to grow and thrive—even in a turbulent environment. The RapidResponse model presented here is by no means the "last word." It is offered as a contribution to the dialogue on the organizational forms that will inhabit the twenty-first century.

Creating the Resilient Organization:
Lesson 1

To survive and prosper in a turbulent environment requires operating as a self-organizing and self-renewing system. Unleashing the forces of self-organization and self-renewal requires operating according to a different set of management "conditions." This new "rapid response" entity is referred to as a *Resilient Organization.*

CHAPTER 2

THE CHOICE IN TODAY'S MARKETPLACE:

Be Quick or Be Dead!

In the 1990's you can go from market dominance to decay in a couple of years. Only the nimble can avoid that fate.

Forbes Magazine, January 4, 1993

As every young Marine going into battle knows, there are only two kinds of soldiers: the quick and the dead. Like the soldier, the North American business leader of the 1990s needs to know that in the future there will be only two kinds of work organizations: those that have the speed and flexibility to respond to the marketplace and those that will get swallowed up in an avalanche of change.

Together, technology and fierce competition are radically changing the business environment. Over the next decade, 3 million businesses and an estimated 30 to 40 million jobs will be at risk. Alvin Toffler, prophetic author of *Future Shock* and *Powershift*, says that "the future division of the world will not be between the North and the South, the East and the West, or the First World and the Third World, *the division will be between the fast and the slow.*"

19

In recent years there has been a proliferation of books warning corporate America of the need to change or perish. Because these books target large corporations, they create an impression that only the "elephants" are endangered. However, the need for speed and flexibility applies just as dramatically to small and medium-sized companies, which make up 98% of all businesses.

Some industries will experience the impact of change more dramatically than others. For example, it is estimated that within five years over 60% of the hospitals in California will close their doors. This trend will spread quickly to the rest of the country. It is the smaller hospitals that are most at risk. In addition, many thousands of small companies that service the aerospace and defense industries have been forced into survival mode by major cuts in Pentagon spending. Even groups that were previously considered invulnerable, such as professional firms or private colleges, now join the ranks of the endangered.

The challenge now confronting established businesses is fundamental: how to be highly adaptive and responsive in a marketplace that is continuously in turmoil. From my experience in working with older organizations, both in the United States and in Europe, I have learned that a change in organizational culture is required. Bringing about this change in core assumptions and beliefs is a difficult and complex task.

THE CHOICE: CHANGE OR PERISH

Three examples, from the files of Deevy Gilligan International, will serve to illustrate the dilemma now confronting business leaders. Names have been changed to protect the privacy of the businesses involved.

The future division of the world will not be between the North and the South, the East and the West, or the First World and the Third World, the division will be between the fast and the slow.

Alvin Toffler

Continental Corporation, a 350-person auto parts maker, has been in the business of manufacturing for over 100 years. When Peter McDonagh was brought in as president by the parent company to modernize operations, he found that the company was steeped in tradition and resistant to change. Although Continental had tried quality circles in the early 1980s, a long history of top-down management prevented meaningful involvement by the people at the bottom.

Other initiatives, including statistical process control (SPC), had brought about incremental improvements in the manufacturing process, but the basic culture remained the same. The company was having great difficulty making changes demanded by the Big Three automakers in Detroit.

> **The problem confronting Peter McDonagh: how to get this company, with its hierarchical management and demotivated work force, to respond more quickly to the changes taking place in the automotive industry.**

Valley Regional Hospital has also been in business for almost 100 years. While this not-for-profit acute care facility has a capacity of 350 beds, its current average in-patient census is 150 and declining at an annual rate of 6%. VRH is in direct competition with another hospital serving the same geographical area. Like 40% of the other acute care hospitals in the state, Valley Regional has operated in the red for the past three years.

Carol Peterson was brought in as CEO by the board of trustees in the hope that she could restore the hospital to financial viability. Peterson knows that VRH, like many other hospitals, had been trying a variety of strategies to stop the hemorrhaging of financial reserves.

At one time the hospital invested heavily in "guest relations" training. However, hospital staff, particularly the care-givers, were uncomfortable with the idea that patients be treated like hotel guests, and eventually the hospitality training effort was abandoned. Nothing remained to show for the investment except dust-covered workbooks, motivational posters, and instructional video tapes. The main beneficiary: the vendor that provided the training.

More recently, another consulting firm was brought in to introduce total quality management. Managers and staff were trained in the statistical tools popularized in the Japanese manufacturing industry. A select group of managers were sent off-site to get special training in the skills needed to facilitate process improvement teams. Eventually, however, the total quality management effort became bogged down under the weight of its own bureaucracy. There were different views as to why the total quality effort had not contributed to an improvement in competitiveness. Some attributed the disappointing results to the fact that the methodology had been originally developed for the manufacturing sector. Almost everyone, including middle management, came to see TQM as another fad that would go the way of previous improvement efforts.

Against this background of unfulfilled promises, Peterson assumed responsibility for leading the hospital into the future. She now finds herself struggling to manage in a health services environment that is undergoing chaotic changes, some driven by new technologies that reduce or eliminate the need for in-patient services.

The problem confronting Carol Peterson: how to get a slow-moving highly bureaucratized institution up to speed to compete in a continuously changing health services marketplace.

National Engineering Services (NES) is a relatively young company, having been founded in the early 1960s. NES grew from the garage of the founder into a national company with $60 million in annual sales. Growth and prosperity came almost exclusively from engineering services provided to contractors for the defense industry. With the end of the Cold War, however, the market for NES services began to shrink. (Indeed, no one had anticipated that the Berlin Wall would fall and that there would no longer be as great a need to test new rockets or missiles.) Suddenly, the managers and technicians needed to find new markets that could use the expertise they had developed during a quarter of a century of doing defense work.

The challenge confronting Roger Owens, founder and CEO, can be summarized in one sentence: how to get NES, with its deeply ingrained Department of Defense "culture," redirected toward commercial markets.

The three companies described here illustrate the problems confronting management of over one-third of all businesses in North America. To survive, management must learn how to play in a business environment where *speed*, even more than quality, is the key to prosperity. *The ability to respond quickly to a constantly changing business environment will separate the winners from the losers.*

Speed is really the driver that everyone is after. Faster products, faster product cycles to market. Better response time to customers.

Jack Welsh, Chairman and CEO
General Electric Company

Evidence that many once successful companies are no longer able to play in the fast-changing business environment can be seen everywhere. Indeed, between 1979 and 1988 there was a 50% change in the *Fortune* 500 list. With less notoriety, the small and mid-sized companies, illustrated by the three businesses just cited, are also disappearing. These enterprises simply lack the speed, versatility, and responsiveness to compete in a world where the only constant is change.

UPHEAVAL IN THE MARKETPLACE

Today, all over the continent, business organizations are struggling with unparalleled challenges. What are the pressures forcing these organizations to change? The more obvious ones include fierce competition, new technologies, rising customer demands, global markets, government regulations, and employees no longer willing to check their brains at the door.

Consider some of the more far-reaching changes taking place:

- New countries and alliances appear almost daily on the map, creating new markets, new production centers, and new competitors.

- Inexpensive desktop and laptop computers can gather and manipulate more information than the largest computers could handle just a few years ago.

- New communication technologies are enabling people throughout the world to communicate with unprecedented ease.

It is obvious that traditional work organizations, with their vertical management and complex work processes, lack the rapid response capability required in today's business environment. Designed for a time when the business environment was stable and predictable, they have great difficulty coping with constant and *discontinuous* change. These organizations could be compared with a Model T Ford that lacked the capability to perform on the modern superhighway. The automatic response of management to the changes taking place has been to delayer, down-size, right-size, offer early retirement, and do outplacement. These strategies—if they deserve to be called strategies—have almost nothing to do with increasing the ability of a business to quickly respond to the marketplace.

The failure to halt the decline in the competitiveness of our work organizations has had a major impact on the national well-being. Public consciousness of this issue has been fueled by Ross Perot's political movement and by increasing expressions of concern by other national leaders. Suddenly, we are awakening to the fact that America has undergone a dramatic decline from its position at the summit of economic power in the 1960s. A more detailed examination of the factors contributing to the loss of competitiveness will be provided in Chapter Three.

The ability to *respond quickly* to a constantly changing business environment will separate winners from losers.

A PROBLEM LOOKING FOR ANSWERS

In addition to the reactive measures referred to above, management has used myriad initiatives designed to improve the performance of traditional work organizations. In fact, management consulting has become a major growth industry with American companies now spending over 7 billion each year on outside advice. Readers of business books spend $500 million annually. The marketplace has become a Tower of Babel, with each guru claiming to have all the right answers; executives beat a path to the Baldridge Award winners with the expectation of finding the secrets of success.

Organizations have sought to regain competitiveness through a variety of improvement programs, including "total quality management," "self-directed work teams," "reengineering," "benchmarking," "time-based management," "the learning organization," "factory of the future," "high-performance work systems," "ISO 9000," and various combinations of these programs. As indicated in Chapter One, none of these programs is capable of bringing about a genuine transformation in the performance of any work organization.

The most visible attempt to improve the performance of mature organizations has involved the introduction of Japanese management using the name "total quality management." (An earlier attempt at introducing Japanese management into manufacturing plants, using quality circles, produced few tangible results.) Total quality management has been viewed as the salvation for all kinds of organizations, from schools and government agencies to hospitals and manufacturing companies. And despite growing evidence that TQM is not delivering on its promises, it has acquired something of the status of "true religion" in management circles.

As the evidence of disappointing results becomes increasingly obvious, executives will, understandably, be reluctant to admit that large investments in TQM have had minimum impact on competitiveness. However, it should be clear that what worked well for the Japanese in the 1950s and 1960s will not necessarily remedy declining American competitiveness in the 1990s. This is not to suggest that quality is unimportant. Rather, in the new game of business quality is comparable to the "ante," which must be "on the table" to even begin to play, and speed of response to the marketplace becomes the *competitive* factor. Traditional TQM programs, designed to bring about *incremental* improvements, do little to increase speed to market and organizational flexibility.

In recent years there has been considerable hype over the value of business process reengineering as a tool for bringing about quantum improvements. This approach, advocated as a means of streamlining work processes, is often little more than a cover for reducing the work force. Implemented with little input from the employees affected by the changes, business process reengineering can have a most damaging affect on morale and performance. More important, this mechanistic approach is not capable of bringing about the kind of cultural transformation that is needed if older organizations are to become "rapid response" entities.

The challenge at the present time is not to do a better job of playing by the old rules but to come up with a new set of rules that are appropriate for the 1990s and beyond. The task of changing older business organizations is made difficult by the *mechanistic mind-set* that can be found among executives and managers. They talk about "rolling out" new reengineering programs or total quality initiatives as if they were discussing the introduction of a new computer or telecommunications system. The idea of the organization as a living system capable of self-renewal is foreign to their thinking. These managers seriously underestimate the complexity of the challenge involved in changing group attitudes, beliefs, and behaviors. However, the core assumptions—what we refer to as *organizational culture* —must be changed if older established companies are to develop the agility and responsiveness needed to outperform competitors. The basic flaw in the many "improvement programs" currently available is that they offer the promise of change without addressing those aspects of organizational culture that must be changed to become a highly flexible and responsive enterprise. The traditional work organization does not need to be repaired: It needs to be replaced by a new organizational form that is more appropriate for the twenty-first century.

THE COURAGE TO LET GO

The basic message of this book is that *revolutionary* changes will be needed to be competitive in the new business environment. Revolution, says *Webster's New Collegiate Dictionary,* is "sudden, radical, or complete change . . . a basic reorientation." Tinkering around at the edges will not be enough to ensure success. The core assumptions on which the organization is built will need to be questioned. There will be a reluctance by some to accept the ideas put forward in the following pages. People tend to prefer a Band Aid to surgery, and radical changes are always resisted by those who find comfort in the status quo.

In each of the three scenarios presented at the beginning of this chapter, the CEO might choose the least disruptive option and simply continue to tinker around with the existing situation: Peter McDonagh could decide to bring in another expert on TQM or process reengineering, knowing that the culture at Continental will remain the same; Carol Peterson could offer a program of training in supervisory skills for the department heads, knowing that merely improving supervision will do little to change the bottom line; Roger Owens could bring in a charismatic football coach to give a motivational talk to managers, knowing that the coach's impact will wear off in 24 hours. Or each of these executives can decide that *revolutionary* changes in organizational culture are needed to increase speed to market and agility. Though there are no easy answers for Peter McDonagh, Carol Peterson, and Roger Owens, they cannot keep playing by these old rules if their organizations are to survive.

I believe we have only recently begun the process of discovering the new organizational forms that will inhabit the twenty-first century. RapidResponse management, as described in this book, incorporates the best of what we now know about creating a high-performance organization. It is not an easy process, and those who will lead the way in implementing the core concepts of RapidResponse management will need the courage to abandon outdated interpretations about what does and doesn't work. The time has come for a paradigm shift. Remember what Einstein said: "No problem can be solved from the same consciousness as created it."

Management needs to stop trying to improve outdated organizations and put energy into creating *new organizations* that have the speed, flexibility, and commitment needed to succeed in today's business environment. They need to create *resilient* organizations.

There is evidence that the process of transformation has already begun in some smaller companies. They understand the stark choice confronting companies that want to be competitive in the future: Be *quick* in responding to the marketplace or be dead!

MARKET RESPONSIVENESS: THE 1990S CHALLENGE

The need to develop business organizations that have a high degree of responsiveness becomes increasingly obvious as we move through the 1990s. This new level of responsiveness will not come from working faster or harder or by doing more strategic planning. *The problem for established companies is that they are stuck in the old way of doing things.* Getting the organization unstuck is both difficult and painful. This explains why many executives are lured by the attraction of the quick and easy fix. Changing the *culture* of an organization is highly disruptive.

The challenges involved in increasing responsiveness differs with each organization. For Continental Corporation the challenge involves producing auto parts faster and better than anyone else in the world, including the Japanese. It requires developing a market-focused culture that puts a priority on listening to the real needs of customers. For Valley Regional Hospital increasing responsiveness involves creating an entrepreneurial mind-set throughout the institution. This requires a reeducation and a redeployment of the work force so that the hospital can move aggressively into the out-patient market. For National Engineering Services the increase in marketplace responsiveness involves helping employees let go of deeply entrenched ways of doing business. A basic reorientation away from Department of Defense and toward commercial markets is required. In all three companies the changes that have been initiated have involved profound *cultural* changes. In each case old assumptions had to be abandoned in favor of a new way of viewing the marketplace. Success in each of these businesses has been largely due to the work undertaken in changing the *attitudes, beliefs,* and *behaviors* of employees. While each of these three enterprises have already begun the process of increasing market responsiveness, there are still strong forces pulling them in the opposite direction. Older organizations are extraordinarily resilient when it comes to resisting any attempts to change culture.

The New *Responsive* Factory

In response to the Japanese threat, General Motors Corporation has spent $7 billion over the past decade in building new plants. These ultramodern production facilities are equipped with the latest technology, including advanced robotics. The decision to build these plants was based on the mistaken assumption that competitiveness in the future could be achieved through the old *mass production* paradigm. The leaders at GM were blinded to the fact that economies of scale have become less important than flexibility.

The age of the *responsive* factory has arrived. It is now possible to link functions such as design, purchasing, production, and marketing into a dynamically responsive environment. This information-driven approach will make it possible, even for large manufacturing plants, to be agile and nimble in responding to changing demands of customers. Electronics are also making it possible for small companies to be linked together to form virtual corporations.

A *BusinessWeek* article (Special 1993 Bonus Issue) identified five characteristics of the responsive factory of the future:

1. *Concurrent everything.* This calls for enterprisewide computer integration, with electronic links to customers and suppliers.
2. *Fast development cycles.* A real-time data base will unite all key functions, eliminating time-consuming paperwork and departmental communications barriers.

3. *Flexible production.* Flexibility will be built into all levels of manufacturing.

4. *Quick response.* Factories will be "on call" to respond immediately to orders from customers.

5. *Commitment to lifelong quality.* In the responsive factory continuous improvement of processes and products becomes part of the culture.

The degree of difficulty in bringing about change cannot be overstated. As indicated , three out of four TQM and business process reengineering programs fail to deliver on their promises. Surveys of senior executives on the impact of major change initiatives in their companies consistently reveal a low level of satisfaction with the results achieved. At this time there is a high degree of cynicism regarding any new change programs that are introduced.

The conclusion to be drawn from this chapter is that the rules of the game of business have now changed radically. While many business leaders are still focused on *quality*, the critical issue for today and tomorrow is the ability to continuously respond in an unstable environment. It is a brand new ball game! The old bureaucratic organization, with its roots in the nineteenth century will not make it in the twenty-first century. Before going on to describe the "conditions" for creating the responsive organization, I will elaborate on the inherent weaknesses of traditional work organizations in Chapter Three.

Creating the Resilient Organization: Lesson 2

Speed, responsiveness, and resiliency are the keys to winning in tomorrow's turbulent and unpredictable environment. The lesson for traditional bureaucratic organizations: Learn how to respond quickly or perish! *Quality* is necessary but not sufficient.

CHAPTER 3

A NEW MODEL FOR WORK ORGANIZATIONS

"I pledge allegiance to the flag . . . ." For many, these words stir up patriotic sentiments. When I repeated these words at the ceremony in which I became a U.S. citizen in 1967, I took pride in knowing that I was becoming a citizen of the country with the most dynamic economy in the world.

It is difficult to comprehend how, within a period of just 25 years, my own pride and optimism and the optimism of most Americans has been replaced by fear and foreboding. While other countries like Japan and Germany have gained competitive advantage, America has been in a state of continuous decline. What caused this decline? Was Douglas McGregor correct when, in 1960, he suggested that the bureaucratic organization contained the seeds of its own destruction? More important, what changes will be needed to regain competitiveness in the global marketplace?

Studies reveal that the fall from preeminence can be attributed to both internal weaknesses and a combination of external pressures.

This chapter provides a brief overview of each of the key factors that has led to a decline in competitiveness. This understanding of *why* older companies have lost the ability to compete will provide a context for introducing the three core principles on which to build a high-performance enterprise. This new approach is called *RapidResponse management.*

THE LOSS OF COMPETITIVENESS

The spectacular decline that has taken place over the past 25 years is the result of a combination of factors. The review of these factors will indicate that what is needed is much more than cosmetic changes. There needs to be a radical transformation in the relationship that exists between the individual and the corporation.

"We are going to hell in a hand basket" is the way one worker described the catastrophic decline in American industrial competitiveness. As already noted, executives and consultants have responded to this crisis with a proliferation of improvement programs, including such imports as quality circles, total quality management, just-in-time inventory management, and ISO 9000. All these efforts are based on erroneous assumptions about the true nature of work organizations and about what it takes to bring about a genuine transformation. New programs tend to create a *bandwagon effect,* making a critical analysis of their usefulness or relevancy difficult.

However, America's declining competitiveness clearly indicates American work organizations are dysfunctional. Furthermore, surveys indicate that over 80% of employees do not identify with the business goals of the organizations for which they work; in many workplaces, a soul-destroying malaise is pervasive.

The first step in solving a problem is to identify its *root causes.* Just as the physician carries out a series of diagnostic procedures before the patient is taken to the operating room and the psychologist leads the client through a process of exploration before coming up with therapeutic recommendations, work organizations must look into the causes of organizational malfunctioning.

Key Point: A clear diagnosis of what is wrong with traditional work organizations is a precondition for building a high-performance enterprise.

Each work organization develops its own unique culture. In Chapter Eleven a more detailed discussion of the powerful role that history and tradition plays in shaping organizational culture will be provided. It will be clear that an older company can become a prisoner of its own past. Here, the objective is to give an overview of reasons why established companies have lost the ability to compete and win in the new business environment. Figure 3.1 graphically shows why the bureaucratic organization has become a dinosaur in the modern business environment. While there is a danger in generalizing about work organizations, as there is a danger in making general statements about human behavior, it can be said that most traditional businesses are affected in some way by each of the following factors:

Factor 1. The management of traditional work organizations is dominated by negative assumptions.

In his 1960 classic, *The Human Side of Enterprise*, Douglas McGregor identified an inherent weakness of traditionally managed businesses when he pointed out that management held workers in low esteem. These managers saw workers as lazy, unmotivated, and needing coercion to be productive. Theory X is the label McGregor gave these negative assumptions. He believed these assumptions had their origins in the oppressive working conditions of the nineteenth century. In contrast to these assumptions, McGregor asserted, was the fact that workers have a natural inclination for work, and will willingly accept responsibility if given the opportunity. He labeled the latter set of assumptions Theory Y. It is the Theory X work environment, with its low expectations, that destroys initiative and creativity.

While few present-day managers openly subscribe to the "workers are dumb and lazy" point of view, Theory X thinking is pervasive in the workplace. As negative expectations become a self-fulfilling prophecy, the work environment soon lacks synergy and commitment. Workers merely go through the motions, and managers feel vindicated in thinking that workers are indeed selfish, lazy, and unmotivated! The impact of these attitudes on a company's competitiveness is obvious.

Factor 2. Traditional work organizations get bogged down in their own bureaucracy.

While outdated Theory X assumptions represent an inherent weakness of the bureaucratic organization, they are by no means the only factor contributing to the loss in competitiveness. The bureaucratic organization itself, with its multilayered hierarchy and cumbersome decision-making processes, was designed for a *stable and predictable* business environment and lacks the speed to market and flexibility needed to be competitive in the 1990s. The analogy of getting an elephant to turn around has been used to describe the degree of difficulty involved. In a world where change is constant and unpredictable, an unwieldy bureaucracy becomes a barrier to competitiveness.

America's business problem is that it is entering the twenty-first century with companies designed during the nineteenth century.

Michael Hammer and James Champy,
Reengineering the Corporation

Factor 3. Traditional businesses fail to see the need for change.

All too often, established companies fail to see the need for change until it is too late. Like a frog that is placed in a pan of lukewarm water, and is slowly brought to a boil without ever realizing it is in imminent danger, many companies do not realize that they are slowly being destroyed. The defense contractor faced with a shrinking market may be lulled into thinking that better days are ahead; the hospital with an annual 6% decline in in-patient census may interpret this trend as a temporary phenomenon. Bureaucratic organizations have great difficulty in making adjustments to a rapidly changing

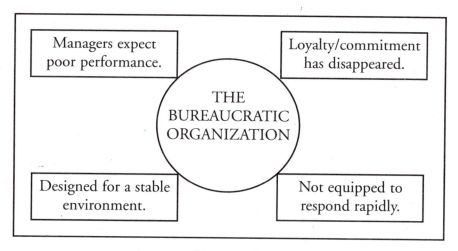

Figure 3.1.
Factors contributing to the loss of competitiveness.

marketplace, especially when the need for change is not very obvious to people on the inside.

In my opinion, there are two kinds of businesses in the United States: those that are heading for the cliff and know it, and those that are heading the same way but don't know it.

Michael Walsh, CEO,
Tenneco

Factor 4. The expectations of workers have changed dramatically.

Another factor contributing to the loss of competitiveness is the changing expectations of workers. In recent years, there has been a tremendous advance in the educational attainment of a majority of people. While 85% of young adults now have a high school education or better, only 53% had equivalent education in 1950. With increased schooling come rising aspirations. Today most workers think of themselves as well educated and entitled to respect for the contributions they make; they want to have a role in designing their own work, to have access to learning opportunities about their field, and to perform their work in a dignified manner. They aspire to esteem and independence.

In addition, many people today are also looking for warmth, meaning, and even fun from the job. There is a basic longing for openness and accessibility not only in private life, but also at work.

Obviously, such aspirations are at variance with the Theory X assumptions that characterize many traditional companies. The structure and management philosophy of work organizations have not kept pace with the changing expectations of workers, and the most basic needs and expectations of the worker go unfulfilled in the bureaucratic organization.

> **The structure and management philosophy of the work organization have not kept pace with the changing expectations of workers.**

Factor 5. Job security has disappeared.

One of the most significant changes in recent years has been *the loss of job security by a majority of workers.* The old social contract between the worker and the corporation has disappeared. The leveraged buyouts, the downsizings, and the rash of mergers have contributed toward the destruction of whatever feelings of security existed among company employees. Slowly and painfully, workers have come to realize that they must *look out for their own interests* as well as the interests of the corporation. Peter Block, the author of *The Empowered Manager*, has referred to this balancing of self-interest with the interests of the corporation as "enlightened self-interest." Employees are no longer willing to commit themselves to the success of their company purely out of a sense of loyalty; they want to know that they are working for themselves as well as for their corporation. Therefore, employee interests need to be taken into account in any discussion of increasing company performance.

When job security goes, employee loyalty to the corporation diminishes. Managers and workers become increasingly preoccupied

The Legacy of the 1980s: A Case Study

The 1980s, with its merger and acquisition mania, served as a wake-up call for employees who had previously placed their financial security in the hands of the company. Employees learned that years of dedicated service counted for nothing when executives needed to slash payrolls to pay off junk bond debt.

The case of Peter is typical. As manager of a small fabric manufacturing company, Peter had done an extraordinary job in building teamwork, morale, and commitment to quality. His plant was a model of what American workers can produce if given the right leadership. All this suddenly changed when the plant was sold by the corporate owner to three Wall Street speculators. The new cash-poor owners set out to squeeze profits at the expense of employees, and morale quickly disappeared. Early one Monday morning two of the owners walked into Peter's office and gave him 30 minutes to get his desk emptied. By 10:00 A.M., Peter was sitting at his kitchen table contemplating the rest of his life. It is experiences like this that have caused so much insecurity among the work force.

about the issue of their own security; workers who were formerly dedicated to the interests of the corporation become cynical and distrustful of management. The business press largely ignored the disappearance of employee loyalty in the 1980s. And the many improvement programs introduced by management in recent years have glossed over the *alienation* of workers. As if it were an irrelevant issue, nobody wants to talk about employee alienation.

The disappearance of employee loyalty in the 1980s is a story that was largely ignored by the business press.

American management, aided and abetted by a platoon of management consultants, continues to perpetuate the myth that workers can somehow be motivated by token involvement. But these managers and consultants fail to appreciate the most important fact about today's workplace: *employee loyalty, trust, and commitment have now largely disappeared.* Employees will not respond to cute slogans and pep talks when they might join the ranks of the unemployed at any time.

Factor 6. There is an increased use of "throwaway workers."

Never before have so many workers been uprooted. It is not just the people at the bottom who have had job security undermined: Over 3 million middle managers lost their jobs in the 1980s, causing widespread insecurity in the managerial ranks. Those who survive the downsizing of businesses must work harder: It is estimated that today's manager works an extra month annually when compared with his or her counterpart of the 1960s. And the work is not getting any more enjoyable. A CNN poll revealed that only 22% of respondents found work hours better than off hours. This statistic represents a complete reversal of opinion from an earlier generation of workers. While the widespread discarding of permanent workers has caused pervasive insecurity among survivors, it has been a bonanza for the outplacement business. Outplacement counselors have become the undertakers of the business community, helping soften what is often a devastating blow. The discarding of permanent employees has given rise to the use of "temps" for all kinds of work. A recent report on the "MacNeil-Lehrer NewsHour" referred to this phenomenon as "the temping of America." Companies hire temporary employees so that they do not have to provide job security or benefits. However, while "throwaway workers" may be good for short-term results, they are not likely to provide a foundation on which to build a high-performance enterprise.

Factor 7. There is an inability to adapt to information technology in traditional organizations.

Another factor that is threatening the viability of traditional work organizations is the impact that information technology is having on the way work gets done. We have only begun to understand the impact of the new computer-based technologies that are making

Broken Promises

The AT&T plant in North Andover, Massachusetts, is a sprawling polished brick and glass complex with sweeping manicured lawns leading up to the main entrance. Inside, work areas are freshly painted, meticulously cleaned and filled with well-dressed technicians and the most modern machines in the business. In the fall of 1992 this plant was the recipient of a coveted prize—the Malcolm Baldridge National Award. A large banner over the main entrance proudly proclaimed this historic achievement to the world. Seven months later, nearly 1,000 at the plant were abruptly eliminated. Many of the "downsized" employees felt a deep sense of betrayal.

Fear is spreading like a contagious disease throughout the workplace. Like survivors of war, many full-time workers today are nearly as ravaged as their fallen comrades—drained of loyalty to a system that, to them, is collapsing all around. For many, there is no longer any sense of security or cooperation. Cynicism is becoming pervasive. One of the employees who was dismissed from the AT&T plant expressed a growing sentiment: "I'll never, never give this kind of commitment to any company again."

Of course the layoff at AT&T is in no way unique. Corporate America is obsessed with downsizing themselves to profitability. The irony is that there is very little evidence to support the use of layoffs as a means of regaining competitiveness. While reducing the work force can lead to short-term corporate profits, the effect on employee productivity is devastating. Loyalty to the company disappears. Workers are becoming increasingly distrustful of the reasons given by management for these reductions. In some of the most reputable companies workers have become scared and bitter.

the old distinctions between managers and the workers less meaningful. We have entered a new age in which employees who work in computerized environments require a much broader knowledge of how systems and processes operate. The impact of the computer on the work environment has been documented by Professor Shoshanna Zuboff of Harvard University in *The Age of the Smart Machine* (New York: Basic Books, 1988). Using case histories, Professor Zuboff describes how the nature of work is changing. In many cases the technology is changing faster than the people who use it are able to change. In industrial environments workers who formerly were engaged in physical activity now find themselves adjusting to a work environment that includes a keyboard and monitor. Making the shift from physical activity to mental activity has not been easy for many of these workers.

In the traditional organization, there was a division between those who had access to information and those excluded from the knowledge base. However, new technologies place a priority on *intellectual activity* at every level. This means that workers need more information to function effectively. When people at all levels have access to the information base, the role of managers as gatekeepers of information becomes outdated.

Organizations have also failed to take full advantage of the computer as a tool for increasing the efficiency of work processes. Faced with the new information technologies, most executives struggle to automate bureaucratic delivery systems that should be obliterated. Again, the old bureaucratic attitudes and practices remain unchanged. The practice of automating old systems is sometimes referred to as paving the cow path: rarely will this automating of a bureaucratic process increase speed to market or customer responsiveness.

Factor 8. There is an inability to respond effectively to increased competition in the marketplace.

Just as the rate of change has accelerated with the introduction of new information technologies, global competition has begun to provide new challenges. A marketplace that was formerly stable and predictable has become chaotic and unpredictable. The changed buying habits of customers, changes in product life cycles, and the demand for increased quality have also contributed to the demand for increased management intensity and faster response to change. Traditional work organizations need to become more market focused.

The overall effect of the rapidly changing business climate is to increase competition and the need for organizational flexibility.

Factor 9. Traditional work organizations promote dependency in the work force.

A more subtle factor negatively affecting the ability of older organizations to compete is the fact that management practices discourage risk taking and entrepreneurial activity. The traditional work organization promotes and reinforces *dependency behavior* at every level. Because employees who are treated as children are not likely to develop feelings of ownership or responsibility, workers get caught in the dependency trap. Eventually, workers become dependent on the directions of management and cease using their own judgment. The use of the time clock is an example of dependency creating management. While managers complain about the immaturity of workers, their own behavior is part of the problem. In employee surveys conducted by Deevy Gilligan International, we found that employees, when asked what they would like to say to their manager, invariably said that they wanted to be "treated as adults."

Employees who are treated as children are not likely to develop feelings of ownership or responsibility.

The subliminal message in bureaucratic organizations is "keep your mouth shut and stay out of trouble." Thus, passive behavior is rewarded while risk taking is discouraged. This creates a cycle of dependency that results in a deadening of the entrepreneurial spirit. The essence of the bureaucratic way of doing business is the tendency to opt for safety, caution, and control. In the bureaucratic environment managers focus their energies on moving up the ladder and are rewarded for maintaining control. They learn to play it safe and to avoid risk taking at any cost. The only real heroes are the people who champion the status quo.

Dependency *destroys the natural enthusiasm and creativity of workers.* One of the consequences of dependency is that workers become expert in pocket-vetoing management decisions. People become good at pretending to work. They withhold commitment. They are willing to exercise the veto, by ignoring management, when they feel their own interests are ignored. Obviously, there is no magic formula for overcoming dependency and building high-performance behavior. In the bureaucratic organization, employees are like prisoners who occasionally succeed in running the prison. Breaking the cycle of dependency cannot be accomplished by managerial edict.

A TIME FOR FUNDAMENTAL CHANGE

What emerges clearly from this discussion of traditional work organizations is the need for *fundamental changes* in the assumptions around which the workplace is organized. Using medical terminology we could say that work organizations are in "critical condition." The symptoms we have identified suggest that much more is needed than some kind of motivational program for employees. Any program designed to transform traditional work organizations into high-performance enterprises would need to address these factors affecting competitiveness:

- Managers who underestimate the willingness of workers to be committed and assume responsibility
- Managers who unwittingly promote immature dependent behavior
- The loss of job security and the resultant decline in employee loyalty and commitment
- The lack of awareness of the need for revolutionary change
- The mistaken belief that massive downsizing will somehow lead to increased performance and productivity
- Cumbersome bureaucracy that prevents fast and flexible responses to change in the marketplace
- The failure to adapt to the new information technologies

What this diagnostic summary does not fully capture *is the extent to which bureaucracy can destroy worker motivation and initia-*

tive. I believe it is important for managers to understand why traditional work organizations negatively impact morale and productivity. This is a question that will be addressed more fully in Chapter Eleven.

WANTED: AN ALTERNATIVE TO THE BUREAUCRATIC MODEL

In Chapter Two I reduced the challenge confronting the management of older organizations to one sentence: Learn how to be agile and responsive or perish. The bureaucratic model is antithetical to the level of responsiveness and flexibility that is needed in an increasingly turbulent environment. As indicated in Chapter One, I offer the RapidResponse model as an alternative to the traditional "command-and-control" approach to managing organizations.

Speed, flexibility, and a high level of commitment are the attributes that distinguish the RapidResponse organization from the traditional bureaucratic organization. Operating in the RapidResponse mode represents a departure from the way businesses have been managed in the past.

The building of the RapidResponse organization involves creating "conditions" that enable employees to become full partners in the enterprise and that allow a free flow of activity in the direction of the customer. As previously indicated, I generally refer to these conditions as the "Three Secrets of RapidResponse management." While these operating principles may appear self-evident, they are "secrets" in the sense that they are outside the existing management paradigm.

RAPIDRESPONSE MANAGEMENT: THE "NEW DEAL"

Taken together, these three "conditions," introduced in Chapter One, constitute *a new deal between the people who own businesses and the people who work* for them. They provide the foundation for building a company that is free of all unnecessary bureaucracy and poised to take advantage of new opportunities in the marketplace. By implementing these concepts, a company can move away from the *control paradigm,* in which workers perform out of a sense of obligation, and toward a new paradigm based on employee commitment in which human potential is maximized and the company is positioned to respond quickly to the marketplace. As already pointed out, the ultimate goal is the development of a business entity that can truly be described as a *resilient organization.*

RapidResponse management captures the essential changes that older companies must make to survive in the new fast-changing marketplace. These three simple but powerful tenets contain the secrets to unleashing the human potential of any business organization. Unlike many of the "quick fix" approaches of recent years, RapidResponse management goes to the heart of what is wrong with traditional business enterprises. The biggest single obstacle to building a high-performance organization is worker alienation. As I have outlined in this chapter, there are a variety of complex reasons for this alienation. Any effort to transform traditional businesses into high-performance enterprises that does not address worker alienation will not succeed. It seems perfectly obvious that without worker commitment, there is no possibility of creating a "rapid response" business enterprise.

> **Any effort to transform traditional businesses into high-performance enterprises that does not address worker alienation will not succeed.**

The second biggest obstacle to transforming an established company into a market-responsive business organization is a combination of bureaucratic procedures and practices. Hierarchical organizations with unwieldy bureaucracies are not capable of making the quick adjustments needed in a dynamic and rapidly changing business environment. Work organizations as we know them were designed in the nineteenth century. After almost 200 years they have become outdated. It is not surprising that these organizations, designed for a stable and predictable environment, would lose the ability to compete in a marketplace where change is the only constant. The various TQM programs that were introduced in the 1980s were based on the premise that traditional hierarchical work organizations could be "improved." These programs failed because they did not recognize the need for a profound transformation in the way businesses are organized and managed. Hierarchical management as we have known it is dead. We now know that what is needed is a fundamental transformation of the structures, systems, and processes that are involved in delivering products or services to the marketplace. There is a need to move from an internally focused *bureaucratic orientation* to an externally focused *process orientation*.

The RapidResponse Game

1. Allow each player to keep score

2. Create a free flow of activity

3. Give each player a stake in the outcome

THE NEW GAME OF BUSINESS

In Chapter One I described the RapidResponse organization as a self-organizing system. In presentations to executives and managers I sometimes use sports metaphors to describe the *psychology* of high-performance organizations. What I try to get across is the idea that people who are just "playing according to the rules" and who feel shackled by bureaucracy will not give the maximum effort to the company.

The new workplace paradigm borrows from principles that are obvious to anyone who has attended a sporting event. *The energy, the flexibility, the responsiveness, and the focus on winning that are evident in the sports arena can be generated in the workplace by changing the rules.* What works on the basketball court or on the hockey rink will work in the office or on the factory floor because human nature is the common denominator.

The three core concepts of RapidResponse management represent a new way of playing the game of business. Just as the rules of soccer are different from ice hockey, the rules of RapidResponse management are different from bureaucratic management. The fact that someone was good at playing by the old rules is no guarantee that he or she will be able to play according to the new rules. However, though many will be reluctant to embrace the new management practices, they will have little choice if they are to keep up with the changes taking place in the marketplace.

It is tempting to compare the way people perform in the sports arena to performance in the office or on the factory floor. In each case a group of people is united together to achieve a common purpose. However, in the sports arena people are much more energized about achieving the goal. I believe the differences can be explained by the fact that the players on the sports team *are performing according to a different set of assumptions* from those held by "players" in the workplace. In one arena the adrenaline is flowing. In the other situation people feel empty. The lesson is this: *If you want to unleash the human potential in the workplace it is necessary to change the rules that govern how people perform.* This is exactly what we do when we introduce the three concepts that constitute RapidResponse management. We change the conditions for performing in a fundamental manner. These new management practices provide the foundation for building an enterprise that has the agility and responsiveness to compete in today's turbulent marketplace.

Creating the Resilient Organization: Lesson 3

The traditional "command-and-control" organization was designed for a stable and predictable business environment. Transforming these older bureaucratic companies and institutions into resilient "rapid response" entities requires a new organizational form based on a different set of management principles. These principles, referred to here as the Three Secrets of RapidResponse Management, contribute towards creating a work organization where *employees are invested in the success of the enterprise and are not shackled by bureaucratic constraints.*

CHAPTER 4

ALLOWING EACH EMPLOYEE TO KEEP SCORE
Secret 1 for Creating the Resilient Organization

Crunch time. That's when the adrenalin flows in a professional basketball game. The scenario is familiar: The score is tied and there are 5 seconds left on the clock. Diehard fans get a special thrill when the game goes into double or triple overtime. It is the *score* that generates the nail-biting excitement. During "crunch time" the players will reach deeply within themselves to respond to a score from the other team. The *scoreboard* plays a vital role in motivating players.

Without the benefit of a scoreboard, a professional basketball game would lack the intensity and competitiveness we have come to associate with professional sports. Players would not be motivated to make the maximum effort. Despite the clear fact that *the scoreboard is an essential component of the game,* in the world of work a majority of employees perform *without the benefit of a scoreboard.* Because they have no specific information on how the company is performing, one of the most basic motivational tools is missing. Therefore, we should not be surprised to find that an overwhelming majority of employees *do not identify* with the business goals of the organizations that pay them a weekly salary. Ask the teller at your local bank how the bank performed over the last quarter, and you are likely to get a blank stare. You'll get the same response from the clerk at the department store or the machinist on the factory floor. Often, for the teacher it is just another day in the classroom and for the civil servant another day pushing paper. How does the employee identify with the organization if he or she has no access to the scoreboard?

It is rare to find a business organization in which management have a good understanding of the importance of sharing business information with the work force. Management ignore something that is obvious to anyone who has ever attended a major sports event: the power of the *scoreboard* in motivating individuals to superior performance. The same psychology that works in the sports arena also applies to the workplace.

The concept of the "learning organization" has gotten much attention in recent years. Most agree that there is an urgent need to retrain the work force to take advantage of the new technologies. However, this training—no matter how extensive—is not a substitute for giving people real business information. It is business information, not technological training, that gets the competitive juices flowing.

EMPLOYEES NEED ACCESS TO THE SCOREBOARD

Ignorance is a deadly disease that can kill any enterprise. Just think about it: If people don't know, they won't understand, and they won't do the right things. People need to be involved in a *meaningful* way if they are to be motivated. They need to feel they are part of something bigger than themselves and to understand how their efforts contribute toward the big picture. The assumption that workers are content to be *treated as outsiders,* without access to business information, is one of the major fallacies of the bureaucratic organization. Despite generations of conditioning, workers really want to know how they are contributing; they want to think of themselves as intelligent insiders. Recently, while waiting in the lobby of a client organization, I casually asked a maintenance worker who was cleaning the floor how she was doing. The response: "Things are really looking up. We were ahead of plan last quarter. Our stock is up 15% from the beginning of the year. We expect to increase our sales over the next six months." This individual, a rare exception, qualifies as an intelligent insider. All employees have a need for access to the business "scoreboard."

The assumption that workers are content to be treated as outsiders is one of the major fallacies of the bureaucratic organization.

THE PRICE OF KEEPING PEOPLE IN THE DARK

The notion that real business information should be the exclusive property of top management can be traced to the beginnings of the industrial revolution. The people who worked in the mills and factories were uneducated and were hired to do repetitive work that required little intellectual activity. It was assumed that management would do the thinking and the workers would follow directions. From the beginning, the industrial enterprise was a two-class organization that had insiders and outsiders. It follows that *if workers are treated as outsiders, they will learn to act as outsiders.* And outsiders are not likely to make the maximum effort. All the so-called improvement programs that have been tried over the past 25 years have conveniently ignored the need for employees to be intelligent insiders with an understanding of the businesses for which they work.

Business and industry have paid a heavy price for keeping people in the dark. Clearly, many of the problems in business today are a direct result of the failure to share information with employees, to show how the work of employees fits into the "big picture." Too often the individual is unable to see beyond the immediate world of the typewriter or the drafting board or the loading dock.

THE SCOREBOARD IS A SOURCE OF WORKER MOTIVATION

In a RapidResponse organization the competitive juices flow because each employee has access to the scoreboard. Employees know what it takes to win in the marketplace. The desire to outperform the competition is the source of motivation. Workers who are intelligent insiders, who understand the realities of the marketplace, don't need glib slogans or pep talks to get motivated. As in the sports arena, the motivation comes from knowing what is needed to win. However, despite all the talk about the need to create a *learning organization*, there has been little effort to educate rank-and-file employees about the "business of the business."

Those executives who have been willing to allow workers to become insiders, with access to real business information, have discovered the powerful motivational impact this strategy can have on performance.

The Power of Business Literacy: A Case Study

An outstanding example of a company that has discovered the power of business literacy to transform the work force is Springfield Remanufacturing Company (SRC) in Missouri. At SRC, financial information is shared with all employees. The story of this blue-collar enterprise first came to national attention through a report on the "McNeil-Lehrer NewsHour." Jack Stack, the chief executive officer, has become a leading advocate of sharing business information. His book, *The Great Game of Business* (New York: Doubleday, 1992), is a primer on how to use business literacy to gain employee commitment.

In the bureaucratic organization, managers most often use coercion and sometimes even intimidation to achieve results from employees. In training courses for supervisors, maintaining control and providing direction continue to be listed as key responsibilities. "Command-and-control" management has dominated business and industry for over 150 years. In contrast, the primary motivator in the RapidResponse organization is *the universal desire to be a winner.* This desire presupposes a knowledge of the business, including profit and loss information, that has not traditionally been shared with the work force. In many companies employees have to rely on the rumor mill or articles in the business pages of the newspapers to get information on company performance. In the RapidResponse organization, on the other hand, employees know how the company is performing vis-à-vis competitors. They have the most up-to-date information on new products or services. They know what is required of them for the company to maintain profitability.

The ability to respond quickly to the marketplace is based in large part on the level of business literacy that exists among employees.

STEPS IN PROMOTING BUSINESS LITERACY

Allowing each individual within the company to keep score is one of the three core concepts upon which the RapidResponse enterprise is built. Putting this concept into practice requires a level of intelligent employee involvement not found in traditional business organizations and depends upon the ability of employees who have been treated as outsiders to begin considering themselves insiders. Practical steps that can be used in creating an organization inhabited by insiders include the following:

1. *Communicate a clear practical vision to every employee.* Management must position the company in the marketplace and make sure that everyone is aware of the company's direction. Employees cannot do business together unless they know what they are striving to accomplish and how each individual can contribute to the common goal.

2. *Share financial information with each employee.* What is required is real numbers that are both comprehensible and interesting. The "financials" are the best measure of how a company is performing. There is no substitute for this information. Sharing business information requires a reeducation of employees so that the profit and loss statements are understood.

3. *Let employees know how the company is performing vis-à-vis competitors.* Just knowing what the competitors are doing can get adrenalin flowing.

4. *Let each employee know how his or her performance contributes to the success of the enterprise.* The ability to make a connection between individual contribution and the success of the company can be a powerful motivator. Clearly, it is easier to make this connection in smaller companies.

5. *Involve everyone in discussing the key questions.* consider these questions: What do we do badly? Where are we vulnerable from competitors? What changes in the economy will affect us? How might our organization be at risk?

The Friday Huddle

The fact that employees can be "turned on" by business information is illustrated by the experience of a New England–based engineering company. On a Friday morning once each month the general manager and the firm's 40 employees come together in the cafeteria to find out the score. This gathering, with its informality and friendly banter, resembles the atmosphere in a sports locker room more than a business meeting. The general manager gives the "big picture." The "financials" are then presented, and the salespeople talk about what is "in the pipeline" and what "deals" are being worked on. It is all very informal. People want to know such things as: How are we doing compared to last year? What was the "bottom line" for the last quarter? What is in the pipeline? Are there opportunities that we should know about? What are our strategic goals? The discussion is about doing business. After 30 minutes all the employees are on the way back to their respective jobs. The Friday huddle is no big deal. Just a way of staying informed.

COMMON MANAGEMENT MISTAKES

While the concept of sharing business information with the work force is simple and straightforward, management can sometimes miss opportunities to gain employee support and commitment. Typical mistakes made by management include:

- *Putting a slant on bad numbers to hide problems.* If the numbers are bad, there is no point in trying to make them look good.
- *Failing to explain the reality behind the numbers.* Some well-meaning managers throw charts and graphs at employees but fail to put the information in perspective.
- *Withholding critical information.* Employees want to know the whole story. If the company is hemorrhaging, employees want to be able to contribute to the solution.

WHAT EVERY EMPLOYEE NEEDS TO KNOW

Some companies hold quarterly, semiannual, or annual events to share business information with employees. The CEO or CFO, with color slides or overhead transparences will do a "dog-and-pony show" for employees. Unfortunately, these carefully staged events often leave employees feeling mystified. What employees need to know embraces much more than the profit and loss statement. A comprehensive program of business literacy should include the following:

1. *Customer requirements.* The wall that exists between employees and customers needs to be removed. Where possible, employees should have the opportunity to interact directly with customers.

2. *Cost structure.* What are the expenses that go into the production of a widget or into the delivery of a service? Workers can contribute to cost reduction when they know the costs that are involved. For example, if shipping costs are a major cause of concern, employees will need to be kept informed on how the company is doing in controlling these costs.

3. *Financial performance of unit/division.* People can more easily relate to the numbers for their own team or work unit. These numbers can also be used to generate a healthy competitiveness between departments and work units.

4. *Competitive data.* The numbers only make sense when they are compared with competitor numbers. It is important to let employees know exactly what they have to do to outperform the

competition. Sharing competitive data brings home the message that the best measure of success is performance against the competition.

5. *Data on individual performance.* One of the key motivators for sales people is that they get financial reinforcement when they are successful. The better they perform the more they are rewarded. This basic psychology can be extended to all employees. A comprehensive program of business literacy needs to help people understand how they are contributing to the success of the enterprise. However, sharing information on individual performance is only part of the story. In Chapter Six I will suggest that giving employees a stake in the financial success of the enterprise is a key factor in building employee commitment.

THE CHALLENGE:
TO BECOME MARKET FOCUSED

A key goal of RapidResponse management is to get employees focused *externally* on the marketplace. Giving employees business information gets them focused on what is going on *outside* the organization. One of the problems with the bureaucratic organization has been its preoccupation with what goes on inside the organization. In the absence of business information employees become focused on internal "turf" issues. To borrow from the Myers-Briggs Type Indicator, a frequently used psychological test, we can say that the bureaucratic organization has a tendency toward *introversion*. The RapidResponse enterprise, on the other hand, can be described as *extroverted*. This focus on the marketplace makes it possible to respond quickly and effectively to a changing business environment.

When people have business information they will tend to act more like owners than employees. The empowerment to act comes from the understanding of the big picture. The employee who can clearly see what is required to win is in a better position to make a positive contribution.

The Big Picture is all about motivation. It's giving people the reason for doing the job, the purpose for working. If you're going to play a game, you have to understand what it means to win.

Jack Stack, CEO,
Springfield Remanufacturing Company

The more educated the work force is about the company, the more capable it is of doing the things required to get better. One of the problems with total quality management has been the failure to give people a real understanding of how improvements in work processes impact on competitiveness. Employees work on improvement teams but fail to see the connection to the big picture. They continue to be focused on microissues. Teaching TQM tools and techniques is not a substitute for business literacy.

The need to respond *quickly* requires access to the knowledge base at every level and does not allow decision making and problem solving up several layers of bureaucracy. Of course employees must have the authority to act on what they learn. In the new business environment it is the educated organization that will have the ability to outperform competitors. Specific strategies for creating the learning organization are provided in Chapter Fourteen.

INFORMATION SHARING REQUIRES A CHANGE IN *CULTURE*

For business information to be shared with everyone, the culture of business organizations must change. One of the cherished cultural assumptions of traditional business organizations is that business information belongs in the executive suites, not on the factory floor. "Over my dead body" was the response of one executive to the suggestion that business information be shared with the work force. Because information is power and managers are reluctant to share power, managers are experts at finding reasons why information should not be shared. "They wouldn't understand" is the most frequently used excuse. Another favorite is: "We can't give out information that might get in the hands of competitors." Each of these excuses is a straw horse. The real barrier to "letting each player keep score" comes from the fact that this idea is outside the old management paradigm. For all these years managers have assumed that competitive information on company performance should be reserved for a handful of people at the top.

While the idea of letting all employees "keep score" seems easy to implement, it requires a change in one of the core assumptions on which the traditional work organization has been built. There is a cultural barrier to be overcome. Chapter Ten and Chapter Eleven will provide specific strategies for bringing about this cultural transformation.

Creating the Resilient Organization: Lesson 4

To win at the game of business in today's and tomorrow's marketplace requires you to have "players" who are both smart and committed. A basic requirement is that each employee understand "the business of the business." We refer to this sharing of business information as the First Secret of RapidResponse management. It is one of the foundations on which to create an organization that is truly resilient.

CHAPTER 5

CREATE A FREE FLOW OF ACTIVITY
Secret 2 for Creating the Resilient Organization

"Your job is to do the lifting, not the thinking." This was the comment made by my supervisor, 30 years ago, to a suggestion I made about streamlining a work process. These words go to the heart of what is wrong with the bureaucratic organization. They reflect a mind-set that emphasizes hierarchical prerequisites and a rigid adherence to tradition.

The modern business environment demands streamlined work processes. The words "free flow" suggest an absence of bureaucratic barriers and needless policies and procedures. Clearly, if an organization is to have a high degree of responsiveness, the employees must be free of hassles and constraints. Employees need to have the same freedom to perform as the player on the basketball court; bureaucracy and complexity are barriers to speed and responsiveness. A lack of flexibility and speed can be fatal in a highly competitive marketplace that is undergoing constant and discontinuous change.

Many older organizations have layers of management that severely interfere with the free flow of activity. Accomplishing a simple task can require negotiating a maze of bureaucratic policies and procedures and endless hours spent in nonvalue-adding activity. While this sense-less bureaucracy is most frequently associated with governmental agencies such as the Department of Motor Vehicles, it can be found in almost every business organization. Examples of crippling time-wasting activity are not hard to find. A few examples from the files of Deevy Gilligan International will serve to illustrate:

- In one large manufacturing plant three weeks and 28 distinct steps were required to get a computer from the engineer's desk to the outside vendor for repair.
- In a community hospital nonvalue-adding activity caused delays of one to two hours in physicians' seeing walk-in patients in the emergency room.
- In one engineering services company needless delay in getting reports to clients was identified as the biggest factor affecting client retention.

As these examples show, work organizations are crippled by redundant activity. In an environment where speed to market is essen-tial, bureaucratic policies and procedures can be life threatening. Old departmental barriers need to be removed to allow a free flow of activ-ity in the direction of the customer. Michael Hammer, coauthor of *Reengineering the Corporation*, advocates obliterating processes that have become overly bureaucratized. What is clear is that older organi-zations will need to eliminate waste, rework, and bureaucratic barri-ers to be able to respond quickly and efficiently to the customer.

BREAK DOWN BUREAUCRATIC BARRIERS

The *structure* of the bureaucratic organization is not conducive to speed or flexibility. Because people in the organization see themselves as members of separate departments—or "silos" of vertical power—they often waste time and energy competing with each other for resources and rewards.

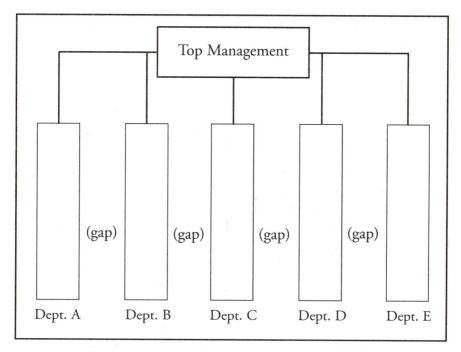

Figure 5.1.
Bureaucratic "stovepipe" organization.

Figure 5.1 shows a traditional *internally focused and vertically managed* organization. Most notably, customers—the life blood of any successful business—are not included in the diagram. Indeed, in this kind of hierarchical environment people are oriented "upward"— toward the chief executive—and communication flows up, rather than in the direction of the customer. It is *the gap* between Department A and Department B, for example, that interferes with the free flow of activity in the direction of the customer. Too often the hand-off between departments results in needless delays and mistakes. When the prime allegiance is toward the department or the function, as in the bureaucratic structure,

- An "us versus them" relationship develops.
- One department can cause the processes of the entire company to malfunction.

- Unmanaged hand-offs between departments often disrupt the continuity of critical cross-functional work processes, creating redundant, sluggish systems that are unresponsive to customers.

While the bureaucratic organization is functionally oriented, as illustrated in Figure 5.1, the RapidResponse enterprise of the future will be *process oriented*. Instead of promoting the vertical flow of information, activity flows across the organization as illustrated in Figure 5-2.

In the figure, the major cross-functional work groups involved in a telecommunications company's product development are diagrammed to illustrate the flow of activity. This series of interrelated activities is called a *Key Business Process*. It is clear from this illustration that the most important activity occurs in a *horizontal* direction, across the bottom of the organizational chart. The new business environment demands that we look at activity as flowing from west to east as in Figure 5.2, rather than from south to north as illustrated in Figure 5.1. Obviously, reducing cycle time involves managing the flow of activity from one end of the Key Business Process to another. Various terms, including "reinventing," "redesign," and "reengineering," are used in describing the task of creating a free flow of activity. In this chapter the process of streamlining key business processes is referred to as *process redesign*.

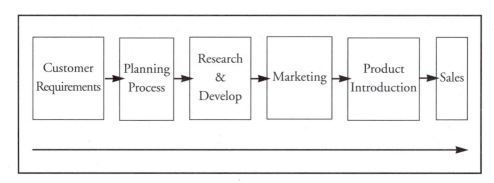

Figure 5.2.
Example of a Key Business Process.

"Reengineer" or "Redesign"?

Reengineer is the term now used to describe efforts to streamline work processes. Implied in the word is the notion that an organization is a mechanical entity that can somehow be manipulated much in the manner that an engineer would manipulate a machine. However, an organization is a *living system*, not an inanimate object. For this reason I prefer to use the word *redesign* in describing activities designed to streamline work processes.

Figure 5.3 shows the flow of activity involved in getting a product to a customer.

A business organization exists to provide a product or service for a customer, not to serve a bureaucracy. Financial success is based on operational excellence. Managing the end-to-end flow of activity in the key business process is one of the requirements for developing a "rapid response" enterprise that can effectively meet the needs of tomorrow's customers.

It is obvious that the people who are involved in the chain of activity across the organization are closer to the customer than is the manager and are therefore in the best position for suggesting ways of improving processes. The role of management is to create an environment where these improvements can take place. While some business organizations remain content to make incremental improvements at

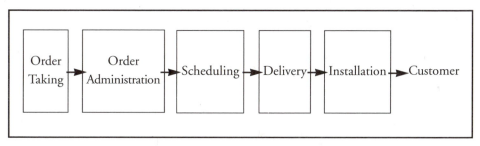

Figure 5.3.
Illustration of order to install process.

different steps in the delivery system using total quality management techniques, a more radical redesign of the whole process from end to end through *business process redesign* will be necessary to achieve dramatic and lasting success.

> *We can only achieve quantum steps of improvement if we get the organization looking at issues in totally new ways. It doesn't help simply to encourage everybody to work harder. The issue is to take a fresh look at problems and concentrate our efforts on core processes that have the largest leverage in improving our position in the marketplace.*

Gerhard Schulmeyer, President and CEO,
Asea Brown Boveri, Inc. (ABB)

In the traditional hierarchical organization, hand-offs between departments are the main source of delay. By definition, a hand-off is nobody's responsibility. To establish legitimate responsibility and follow-through, the "owners" of the various groups in the chain need to make sure hand-offs are made quickly and effectively. Employees, by their closeness to the work process and to the customer, have the knowledge to make suddenly needed adjustments in the delivery system.

STREAMLINE THE ORGANIZATION

For at least a decade, American business and industry have recognized the need to reduce bureaucracy and increase the efficiency of work processes. However, as noted earlier, the various quality initiatives that have been introduced have produced minimum results. These initiatives, based on Japanese management and emphasizing incremental improvement, invariably add to the existing bureaucracy. Business process redesign, as described here, is a more direct, simple, and efficient approach to streamlining work processes. Employees can be involved with a minimum of training. The people who do the work, the "owners," put the current process under the microscope to identify waste, rework, disconnects, and nonvalue-adding activity. They develop a *process activity map (PAM)* that illustrates end-to-end work flow and includes a description of what happens at key points in the process.

After the current work process has been studied and analyzed, the next step is to redesign wasteful activity out of the process and to enhance work flow. New information technologies, such as pen-based and wireless computing, can help increase speed and efficiency by eliminating paperwork.

Because new information technologies are radically changing the way work gets done and making speed the key factor in business success, every business organization will need to undergo a redesigning of key business processes if they are to survive and prosper into the twenty-first century. For example, an invoicing process that was "invented" in the 1950s will need to be redesigned for the 1990s.

Case Study:
Redesigning a Billing Process

The community hospital in a small northern New England town, with its traditional management culture, was faced with a rapidly declining in-patient census and the need to increase market share. Administrators and department heads went off-site to work at positioning the hospital in the local health services marketplace. The resulting vision statement included the goal that the hospital would become the preferred provider for area residents. This process led to discussion of what key business processes would need to be redesigned to achieve the goal. It was clear that late and inaccurate billing charges affected not merely cash flow but also the image of the hospital in the community. A team, which included individuals who had ownership for key steps in the process, was formed to put current processes under the microscope and to construct a process activity map. Experiments were conducted to pilot test new processes. As a result, efficiency was increased by 50%, rework was reduced, interdepartmental communication was improved, and late charges were eliminated. All these accomplishments were carried out with no fanfare and at minimal cost.

PROCESS REDESIGN:
SOME KEY REQUIREMENTS

The redesigning of key business processes as a strategy for creating free flow implies a major *streamlining* of the bureaucratic organization. The issue of how to *overcome resistance* to these changes will be explored in later chapters. The following requirements should be kept in mind when considering the use of business process redesign as a means of eliminating bureaucracy and increasing free flow.

1. The redesigning of key business processes begins with the creation of a practical vision for the future.

In professional sports each team knows exactly what it wants to accomplish. Similarly, in business, management must position the organization in the marketplace and make sure everyone is focused in the right direction. As pointed out in Chapter Four, a practical vision stimulates increased business literacy throughout the organization and serves to clarify which work processes need to be redesigned. If the practical vision is to become "the preferred provider of health services in the North Country," then key processes that contribute to this vision will be the focus of redesign activity. Similarly, if the practical vision for an accounting firm is to "provide timely reports to clients," the focus will be on those processes that contribute to this vision. *In each case the practical vision becomes the rationale for all activity designed to create free-flowing delivery systems.*

In traditional bureaucratic organizations, enormous energy is wasted on activity that has nothing to do with winning in the marketplace. The practical vision makes it possible to get employees focused beyond internal concerns and to concentrate their energy on those processes that are essential to delivering the product or service to the market. The practical vision also provides a rationale for revising company policies and procedures. In the RapidResponse enterprise, the entire infrastructure supports employees in pursuit of a shared goal.

2. Process redesign requires that managers get out of the way.

In the bureaucratic organization, managers become invested in protecting their "turf" and in preserving the status quo. Streamlining those Key Business Processes that cross departmental boundaries requires the cooperation of middle management. In the Rapid-Response environment the role of the manager is analogous to that of the coach in professional sports. It involves coordinating the efforts of the different "players" and negotiating hassles that might interfere with performance. The *effective* manager encourages employees to cut waste, redundancy, and other nonvalue-adding activity out of the system. In the RapidResponse enterprise employees are empowered to eliminate rework and other wasteful activity without having to fight against an obstructionist managerial bureaucracy.

3. Process redesign requires direct involvement of the process owners.

Employees in a particular field know better than managers or consultants how to identify opportunities to improve the work flow and the quality of the product or service delivered.

The Five Thousand Dollar Envelope!

The president of a small Southern bank asked a consultant to develop ideas on ways to make his institution more user friendly. In particular, the president wanted ideas on how to redesign the lobby area to ensure a favorable first impression. The consultant, in a casual conversation, asked several employees what changes they would make. It was a question they had already considered. One employee took an envelope and proceeded to outline what the redesigned lobby would look like. The consultant, realizing that he was looking at the creation of what was, in reality, a $5,000 envelope, asked the employee why she hadn't shared her valuable suggestion with the president. "Nobody asked," was the response. This anecdote illustrates an important truth: *The people closest to a job are almost always the best source for answers.*

---

4. The focus of business process redesign is process simplification.

Flow-charting current processes and using information technology to enhance process flow will bring about quantum improvements in product and service delivery. Process redesign increases efficiency, reduces cost, and enhances quality. End-to-end flow-charting identifies the nonvalue-adding steps.

5. Business process redesign requires a transformation of the entire infrastructure.

The redesigning of key business processes needs to be accompanied by a reduction in bureaucratic policies and procedures. The organizational infrastructure needs to be replaced. In New England, some old abandoned factories have been converted into upscale condominiums and office buildings. This conversion has required a new infrastructure consisting of heating, air conditioning, elevators, and other support structures. Similarly, older companies and institutions need to undergo a "renovation." If the personnel manual has created unnecessary obstacles for employees, the manual will need to be revised or eliminated. Decision making and problem solving should be pushed to the lowest possible levels so that communication across departmental boundaries may flow freely and without obstruction. Some layers of the hierarchy may need to be eliminated to speed up decision making and problem solving.

In the bureaucratic organization employees spend so much time jumping through bureaucratic hoops that they have little energy left for customers. The organization becomes stifled under the weight of bureaucratic rules and regulations. This restrictive bureaucracy is encountered everywhere—in doctors' offices, in governmental agencies, on the campuses of major universities, in the customer service departments of retail stores, at the telephone company. The list is endless. Employees become conditioned into using "policy" as a reason for frustrating clients or customers. This infrastructure of policies and procedures, bolstered by the obsession to maintain *control,* can be found in most traditionally managed organizations. "Sorry, there's nothing I can do—it's company policy," is a common refrain in the marketplace.

The major obstacle to creating free-flowing work processes is management resistance. Although the task of process simplification is relatively easy and requires only minimal training, maintaining *control* is part of the bureaucratic paradigm. The strategies for overcoming resistance and achieving a cultural change will be discussed in Chapter Twelve.

6. Process redesign goes beyond "paving the cow path."

Business process redesign is a *radical* process, designed to create free-flowing work systems. Information technology is used to streamline and increase speed to market. Everything that would get in the way of free flow is ruthlessly eliminated. The effort goes below the surface to get at delays, rework, disconnects, and all forms of nonvalue-adding activity. The old process may have been formed like a cow path, with lots of winding steps and detours. This path should not be repaved, but eliminated: The new information technologies have made it possible to create new key business processes that are faster and more direct than the old cow path.

THE STEPS IN CREATING FREE-FLOWING BUSINESS PROCESSES

The use of business process redesign to create free-flow is not a one-time event. Older established companies and institutions will need to engage in a continual redesign effort over a period of several years. Despite the amount of activity necessary for eliminating bureaucratic practices, business process redesign is relatively easy to use. There is no major up-front investment in training or outside consultants. The redesign of a Key Business Process, illustrated in Figure 5.4, can be carried out in six sequential steps:

Step 1. Identify key processes to be improved.

All processes chosen for redesign should relate to the *business goals* of the company. It is important that the initial definition of project objectives include the perspective of all appropriate managers. I have found that differences often exist even among those people who

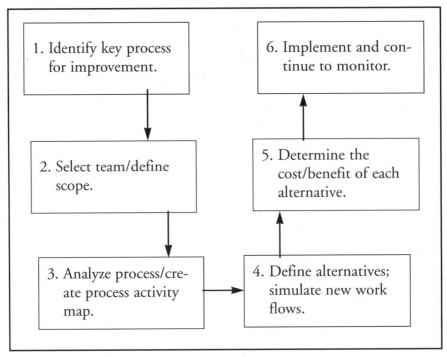

Figure 5.4.
Six-step strategy for redesigning Key Business Processes.

agree with the necessity for the change. By getting input from every-one, and setting honest expectations and objectives, a consensus can be developed. Clarifying the expectations of managers will prevent problems at a later stage. It is useful at the beginning to establish the length of time and approximate cost that will be necessary to com-plete the project.

Every redesign effort will be performed to meet one or more objectives. As indicated, each objective is tied to a business goal and therein derives its reason for existence. Typical requirements for a redesign project include

- Cutting the time it takes to do something
- Improving a service, such as customer support
- Solving a problem, such as mistakes in billing

These requirements determine the focus of the redesign effort. They are also the factors against which success will be measured. It is very important that managers concur that the effort is worth making and that they agree on success criteria. I recommend the development of a written project definition that is shared with all managers who will be impacted by the redesign project.

The initial project should have a high probability of success. It is better to start with a project that has strong management support, is clearly defined, and is capable of producing "bottom-line" results. Of course, all subsequent projects must also be justifiable from a business perspective.

Step 2. Select a team made up of process owners.

The composition of the team working on the redesign project will be determined by the scope of the project. The scope is the boundary of the process that is to be redesigned; it is not defined by *organizational* boundaries. Furthermore, the project must encompass an entire process: While all the work flow of a process may not be changed, it must be included within the scope of the project. Setting scope can require considerable up-front discussion. Unfortunately, managers have been conditioned to see problems through *organizational lenses* rather than as activities that flow horizontally across several units or departments. The nature of a Key Business Process, such as responding to an order from a customer, calls for activity that takes place in several departments. The scope should be broad enough to provide real benefit, but focused enough to be controlled. Highly complex processes can be redesigned after the company has gained experience in using this tool.

As already indicated, processes in traditional hierarchical organizations are arbitrarily divided along organizational lines, although the process work flow is known to cross these lines frequently. The boundaries of this flow, not organizational boundaries, are used to define the scope of the project. In complex organizations the scope of the process redesign will always include several departments. *Each key department or work unit through which the process flows must be represented on the team that is organized to do the redesign work.* If a key group in the chain of activity that makes up the Key Business Process is not represented on the team, they are not likely to be committed to the proposed changes. It is sometimes necessary to add one or two members as the project progresses and the full scope of the effort becomes more fully understood.

Step 3. Create a process activity map illustrating what happens from end to end.

This step involves developing the information that will be required and analyzing the work flow. This task involves scrutinizing the policies, business rules, costs, values added, revenues, work flows, organizational structure, job definitions, production processes, and computer systems that are related to the process. The end-to-end flow of activity is put under the microscope. The familiarization process requires an intensive effort on the part of the team. This step is, however, the *foundation* for redesigning the process. Step 3 develops fully detailed maps of current processes to enable new processes to be designed. This is the step that must identify all the problems with the way things are being done. The process activity map will identify all the activities, relationships, and problem areas in the work flow. It will include information on rework, disconnects, and all nonvalue-adding activity. In many cases, existing quality assurance data will be available for use by the redesign team. The process activity map will include not merely a flowchart but notations on all aspects of the process.

Step 4. Define alternatives; test new work flows.

Alternative new processes are designed in this step. At this point the work flow and process analyses performed in step 3 are used to create new process and operations designs and to simulate the new operation. The change team is responsible for creating the new process designs.

In projects that cross organizational boundaries it is important to involve all managers in the process simulations. Their participation includes advising and providing insight into the corporate culture and the peculiarities of their operations. The pragmatic input of the managers is essential if the project is to be successful. By direct participation, the department managers have the ability to add to the impact of the project. If a key manager is left out during this experimental stage, he or she may sabotage implementation.

The redesign team usually does not have difficulty producing new design alternatives for each process. The work is done using trial and error, but the choices are generally clear if the current operation and its supporting systems have been well researched. The redesign team should solicit input from employees and both internal and external customers. Project participants can apply everything that they have learned about what works and what does not work in the company.

The process activity maps for a single process design alternative will be redrawn several times. The new designs will address the projects' changing goals and will reflect both the support available from technology and the corporate culture. Creativity is the principal ingredient in carrying out this step. However, change should never be made unless it significantly improves something. The question to ask is: Do these changes *reduce complexity and increase process flow?*

It is important that the workers who perform the business functions that are being changed participate in the job redesign activities. Simply informing departmental managers of the proposed changes is not adequate. The participation of workers provides invaluable insight. It also helps promote acceptance and commitment.

Sometimes changes in the *organizational structure* will be needed to maximize the benefit of the new process design. Clearly, any changes in structure will need the active involvement and support of top management. If the redesigned process is highly fragmented, significant gains can be made in combining the activity into a new business unit. Consideration should be given to having someone with overall responsibility for what happens from one end of the key business process to another.

The initial analysis of the new design is performed by creating a new process activity map. Questions to be asked at this stage include

- Does the change make good business sense?

- Does the change address the goal of the project?
- Does the change eliminate redundancies and rework?
- Is the technology fully utilized?
- Are the hand-offs between individuals/work groups effective?

Step 5. After experimentation, select the best alternative.

Selection of the best alternative is based on a cost-benefit analysis. The first step in defining both costs and benefits is to confirm the team's understanding of the results of the redesign project. The exact extent of the change that the new design will cause must be defined, and each change to a work flow, process, job, or support must be considered.

There are two different types of costs associated with each new design: the one-time cost of implementation and the continuing cost of operation. Implementation costs include personnel overhead costs, computer costs, and retraining.

Some benefits of redesign will be tangible, while others will not. Certain benefits can be quantified, such as cutting costs. However, intangible benefits like increased customer satisfaction may have the most significant long-term effects. For example, the elimination of customer complaints may take months or years to quantify. *In redesigning processes, it is often the intangibles that provide the most compelling reason to implement a new operational design.*

Where possible, a dollar value should be assigned to each benefit. However, some activities may be viewed as investments in a long-range corporate strategy, such as increasing market share. Some executives, with the mechanistic mind-set, mistakenly believe that the most significant organizational improvements are always measurable.

Step 6. Implement and continue to monitor.

The selection of the best alternative will be related to benefit and cost. One nonfinancial benefit relates to the ability of the new design to make jobs easier and free staff from mindless drudgery. This will improve loyalty and morale and ultimately improve performance. The cost-benefit analysis is the starting point of the implementation plan.

Case Study:
Creating Free Flow in a Hospital Emergency Room

The management of a New England–based municipal hospital was concerned about the negative perceptions of the emergency room among key stakeholders. These perceptions, including complaints of long waits, led management to hire a consultant. After assessing the situation the consultant reported that the problems were the result of negative attitudes among staff. The administrators, having been introduced to the concepts of Edwards Deming, were reluctant to accept "employee attitudes" as the root cause of the problem. A team of process owners, including representatives from admitting, the emergency room, respiratory therapy, laboratory, and radiology, was formed. The task of the team was to develop an end-to-end process activity map. The team looked at everything—work flow, disconnects between departments, information technology, the physical environment, and communications. Comprehensive ideas for streamlining the process were developed within two months. The reception area was refurbished to make it more user-friendly. The need for more cooperation between departments was identified, and follow-up training sessions were conducted. In the process of redesigning service delivery, management and employees came to an understanding of how the work processes were impacting on "customer" perceptions. The "employees' attitudes" identified by the consultant as the problem were merely a symptom of work processes that did not work very well.

Implementing the changes associated with redesign projects is a complicated undertaking. There is a *political* dimension to changing established work processes. The most difficult part of the change—getting people to buy in—will be addressed fully in Chapters Nine, Ten, and Eleven. In a properly executed project, the personnel who will be affected will have worked with the change team, first, to define the old operation and, then, to redesign it. This participation at the design stage breaks down barriers to successful implementation and provides a type of ongoing training. At this implementation stage the staff should have a firm understanding of the new operations and how they fit into it. A failure to involve managers and staff during the design stage will almost certainly lead to failure during the implementation stage. The 80% failure rate of current "reengineering" projects can be largely explained by the failure to consider the *human relations* aspects of implementation.

A detailed implementation plan must be developed that addresses every action necessary to build the new operational environment. All tasks necessary to move the old way of operating to the new one must be defined at a detailed level and then laid out on the schedule. These tasks may include acquiring new computer hardware and software or reconstruction of the physical environment. The involvement of people who are familiar with the capabilities of information technology is essential.

The implementation plan must be flexible enough to be changed as the need arises. The business environment is dynamic, and operational realities change constantly. The process redesign team continues to monitor after implementation. As the changes are implemented team members become reoriented toward the goal of continually improving the performance of the process.

THE KEYS TO SUCCESS

A few basic considerations should be kept in mind to ensure a successful conclusion of redesign projects. Management should remember that process redesign is intended to be used as a tool to produce quantum improvements.

The success factors listed here are based on real life experiences.

1. *Get the strategy straight first.* Take a good look at what business you want to be in and how you intend to make money at it. Before you start improving operations you must first formulate the business strategy. This strategy will tell you which core processes need to be redesigned.

2. *Lead from the top.* Business process redesign is a cross-functional activity. To be effective, the redesign effort must be led by someone whose authority crosses all the functions and who can oversee the process from end to end.

3. *Create a sense of urgency.* Fear, resistance, and cynicism are inevitable as the redesign team begins to unearth problems and toss around radical ideas for solutions. Managers tend to get defensive about what happens in their turf. The case for radical changes in work processes must be made in such a way as to convince key stakeholders. If people are able to see these changes as an absolute requirement for business success, they are more likely to be supportive. The case for change must always come from the marketplace.

4. *Design from the outside in.* The redesign process begins with the customers. The question to ask is: "How do they want us to deal with them?" Keep the focus on major processes that really matter to the customer, not on activities that are of little consequence. The benchmarking of key competitors can provide valuable data as management decide which processes to redesign.

5. *Provide training as needed.* The experience of Deevy Gilligan International is that employees can learn how to create process activity maps with only minimal training.

6. *Involve both management and line staff on the team.* If key managers are not directly involved, they should be kept fully informed from the beginning.

7. *Include expertise on information technology on the team.* New technologies, including pen-based and wireless computing, offer the possibility of greatly reducing work content in key business processes. Information technology expertise needs to be at the table.

8. *Manage you consultant.* Don't let the consultant take control of the redesign project. Control expenses by using the consultant to train internal people to do the work. Be sure to check references before retaining the services of any consultant.

THE CHALLENGE: GETTING STARTED

The second secret of RapidResponse management—the creation of a free flow of activity—involves much more than a tune-up of the old organization. It involves a major reconditioning of systems, processes, and procedures. These changes will not be accomplished easily.

Any effort to redesign work processes will provoke fears on the part of management and workers. Managers will be concerned about losing control. Employees will fear the loss of jobs as efficiencies are introduced. Both managers and employees will need to overcome assumptions about how the workplace should be organized. Introducing the second secret of RapidResponse management requires a *cultural transformation*. A company that focuses exclusively on the *mechanics* of streamlining without dealing with the cultural issues can expect disappointing results. There must be a willingness to deal with the legitimate security concerns of employees. The first priority should be to redeploy personnel whose jobs are eliminated as a result of the streamlining. As Key Business Processes are simplified the hierarchical structure will be flattened and employees will need to become more skilled in working in a team-oriented work environment. This may require training in the skills needed for teamwork.

The question of how to get an established work organization to embrace new cultural assumptions will be addressed in later chapters. The key is to "break the ice"—to get the process started. An understanding of the psychological dimensions of change is an essential first step in bringing about a cultural transformation.

Creating the Resilient Organization: Lesson 5

In a turbulent fast-changing marketplace, the organization must be capable of responding quickly without the constraints of bureaucratic policies and procedures. Activity must flow freely in the direction of the customer. We refer to this streamlining of work processes as the second secret of RapidResponse management. It is one of the foundations on which to build an organization that is truly responsive and resilient in adapting to a changing environment.

GIVE EACH INDIVIDUAL A STAKE IN THE OUTCOME:
Secret 3 for Creating the Resilient Organization

"Every worker is *secretly* an entrepreneur." These are the words a union steward used in explaining the unfulfilled aspirations of members. However, in the bureaucratic organization, there is very little opportunity or incentive for entrepreneurial endeavor. By failing to appeal to the self-interest of lower-level workers, businesses miss out on an opportunity to increase productivity through increased loyalty and dedication. While previous generations of workers may have been content with a fixed wage, today's workers must have a stake in the outcome of their work to feel committed to the company. Remember: Without a high level of commitment a high-performance enterprise cannot be created.

One of the cornerstones of the RapidResponse organization is *enlightened self-interest*: the recognition that people are much more motivated to perform when they are working on their own behalf. Workers will be more willing to contribute to the enrichment of the corporate entity if they know that in the process they are enriching themselves.

THE PAYCHECK:
A REWARD FOR SHOWING UP

Since the days of the industrial revolution the basic wage has been the accepted way of compensating workers. Over time it became an *entitlement* that had very little impact on performance or productivity. When the enterprise was successful in the marketplace, it was the investors and senior managers who were the primary beneficiaries. Worker commitment was derived not from a sharing of profits, but from a *security that went with the job*. However, as I have noted, the old social contract between the worker and the corporation, with its promise of security, has disappeared. The "downsizing" of even the most prestigious corporations in recent years has made employees realize that there is no paternalistic corporation to look out for their interests; they must assume *personal responsibility* for their own financial security.

If people feel that there is no direct relationship between their own efforts and the amount of compensation received because their compensation is fixed by the weekly paycheck, they have little incentive to give the maximum effort. Many company executives fail to understand that token gifts, including Thanksgiving turkeys and anniversary watches, are no substitute to having *a genuine stake in the success of the venture*. The employee who takes the turkey home to the family does not have the same interest in increasing profits as the individual who owns a hundred shares of stock. Certainly, it is not enough to give a "piece of the action" to upper-level executives. Every employee has a built-in sense of fairness and equity, and workers are quick to recognize "downsizing" that is carried out to ensure end-of-year executive bonuses.

A NEED TO REGAIN EMPLOYEE COMMITMENT

Employee commitment can be regained by creating a system whereby the individual shares in the success or failure of the enterprise. When employees have a vested interest, they *act as if they were owners*, and this feeling of ownership is a key ingredient of the RapidResponse enterprise. Commitment is based upon the common interest of people achieving prosperity together.

> **Key Idea: The whole organization needs to be unified and motivated around the common interest of winning in the marketplace. Good customer service comes naturally to the person who has a vested interest in the success of the enterprise.**

SHARING THE SPOILS IS GOOD BUSINESS

Far from being a form of workplace socialism, offering all employees a financial stake in the success of the enterprise makes very good business sense. A well-kept management secret is the fact that companies that have some form of employee ownership or profit sharing consistently *outperform* companies that compensate people with a basic wage. Sharing with employees represents an improvement in capitalism; when people act as owners, the company generates more revenue, and the process benefits them and the stockholders.

If you all own the company together, the wealth that is being created . . . is to be shared. That to me is very powerful. As a front-line worker, that is very very important.

Robert Zicharo
Conference on "The Future of the American Workplace";
quoted in the *Boston Globe*, July 26, 1993

While textbooks on management tend to down-play money as a motivator, it is clear that lack of ownership has a negative impact on motivation. Common sense suggests that "a stake in the outcome" is a prerequisite for building the high-performance organization. Giving workers ownership increases accountability and commitment. The analogy of tenants in a public housing project can be used: A lack of ownership has a negative effect on the way buildings are maintained. This same negative dynamic can be found in work organizations.

COMPENSATION MUST BE LINKED WITH *PERFORMANCE*

The idea of sharing ownership with employees calls for a radical shift in the mind-set of management. At a practical level, giving employees a "stake in the outcome" requires a major transformation of the compensation system. The key is to develop a system that links the performance of the individual or the team with marketplace performance as closely as possible. Employees need to know that the work they do is directly related to the compensation they receive. In recent years there has been some experimentation in the effort to create compensation systems that incorporate the concept of profit sharing. At this time, however, no one "best" system has been identified.

Innovative companies are searching for systems that recognize that wealth is created at every level of the organization and that there should be a more equitable sharing of resources. There is a growing understanding of how compensation can be used as a way of *building* an organization. The fact that so many work "just for the money" says something about a pervasive cynicism that can be found in many companies and institutions. A compensation system that includes *all employees* in ownership contributes toward rebuilding morale by giving people a sense of purpose.

LACK OF LINKAGE BETWEEN COMPENSATION AND STRATEGY

Compensation experts agree that employee compensation systems should flow from the mission of the company. However, that rarely happens in traditional compensation systems. In recent years there has been a trend to develop programs that consist of the following two elements:

1. *Fixed compensation.* This is the base pay for time spent working for the company.
2. *Variable compensation.* This is the financial compensation distributed apart from base pay. It is usually tied to some specific improvement.

Traditional approaches to *base pay* establish no real linkage with the company's mission or with the strategy of the company. These compensation systems simply don't include a process for establishing the connection between pay and strategy.

Companies are doing a better job of linking *variable compensation* programs with strategy. Many of these programs focus on specific improvements and are easier to measure. They are more likely to be aligned to strategic objectives than the base pay. Too often, however, bonus-type programs are add-ons—they lack proper focus, alignment, and integration with the strategic objectives of the company.

With a few exceptions, there has been little change in employee compensation since World War II. The focus of human resources professionals has been on legal issues, statistical formulas for calculating pay, and job evaluation that permits microscopic evaluation of jobs. These professionals have become very invested in their statistical tools and formulas. They are reluctant to change. Part of the reason for this reluctance is that change is both difficult and painful.

It is not just the human resource professionals who are reluctant to challenge existing practices. Employees in general are reluctant to embrace changes in the way they are compensated. The emotional nature of pay and its relative complexity make it difficult for companies to want to change.

A FLAWED VIEW OF COMPENSATION

The real problem is a flawed view of compensation as an end in itself rather than as an integral part of the strategic direction of the company. Unfortunately, this flawed view doesn't reinforce the flexibility or responsiveness needed in the new business environment. It fails to align or integrate the human assets of the company in support of strategic objectives and is part of a nonvalue-adding process that does little to gain employee commitment.

Quite often, companies introduce improvement programs, such as total quality management, with the *promise* of some form of gain sharing. Somehow, however, these companies never get around to addressing the compensation issues: It is much easier to teach people how to do fish-bone diagrams or Pareto charts than to institute a system that "gives each employee a stake in the outcome."

The old narrowly defined job descriptions are outdated. Because the new competitive marketplace demands cross-functional activity and a greater use of teams to accomplish goals, change in employee compensation systems is inevitable. The old system has its roots in the bureaucratic organization and reinforces narrow job specialization. *What is urgently needed is a new compensation system that reinforces flexibility, teamwork, and market-focused activity.*

THE COMPENSATION PARADIGM IS SHIFTING

It is clear that traditional compensation programs do little to give people a feeling that they have a direct investment in the success of the enterprise. As indicated, base pay is established without consideration of strategic business objectives. The core assumptions underlying compensation practices have gone unquestioned for many years. There has been some experimentation in generating worker commitment by offering some stake in the success of the enterprise. Generally, such experiments involve rewarding specific improvements rather than sharing pretax profits. Nevertheless, some companies have demonstrated that such forms of sharing can provide powerful leverage in building a high-performance enterprise.

The most noteworthy attempts to give employees an investment in the business include the following:

1. Employee stock option plan

Employees are given equity in the company. The employee stock option plan (ESOP) is particularly effective when combined with an educational program that gives employees a good knowledge of "the business of the business." Stock ownership increases accountability. Clearly, when employees act as if they "own the place," the business will be more successful.

2. Gain sharing

As the name implies, gain sharing involves paying employees a bonus based upon improvements in the operating results of an organization. Many organizations are discovering that when designed correctly, gain-sharing plans can contribute to employee motivation and involvement. Employees are rewarded for specific gains in productivity and cost-cutting. The key is to design a program that is considered fair by both management and employees. This requires that employees trust management's motives. If management pushes up the standards, so that last year's gain becomes this year's base, the plan will end up demotivating people. Likewise, if the base in which gains are made stays constant, bonuses quickly acquire an "automatic" component and lose their initial motivating effect. A happy medium must be found to make gain sharing work.

3. The Scanlon Plan

The Scanlon Plan is the "granddaddy" of gain-sharing programs. Named after Joe Scanlon, a union leader in the mid-1930s, the Scanlon Plan is both an incentive plan and a management philosophy. Scanlon believed in a participative philosophy in which managers and workers share information, problems, goals, and ideas. Moreover, he felt that a company's pay system should be tied to that philosophy by rewarding cooperation and problem solving. Based on these beliefs, the Scanlon Plan uses a participative suggestion system involving different levels of worker-management committees. The committees solicit employee suggestions, assess them, and see that promising improvements are implemented. The bonus resulting from savings is often split evenly between the company and the employees. Herman Miller, the furniture company, is sometimes cited as an example of a company that has used the Scanlon Plan to increase quality and return on investments while simultaneously increasing employee benefits. Donnelly Mirrors is also widely recognized as a company that has effectively used the Scanlon Plan to build strong employee loyalty and commitment.

4. Profit sharing

A well-developed profit-sharing program can be a powerful tool for motivating the entire work force. An effective program communicates goals in the most effective way possible—by rewarding people for their achievement. Such a program says to people, "These goals are so important we'll give you a reward if you reach them." This is a way to send a strong message to employees. You give people a challenge and a very good reason for working hard to achieve it. Profit sharing allows employees to share directly in the success of the company. There is no sharing when there are no profits.

5. Special bonus programs

These programs are more likely to have a motivational impact if employees at *all levels* participate. Too many companies limit bonuses to the upper levels of management. In addition, the motivational value of the bonus is often lost by the failure to establish links between individual performance and payment of bonuses. For bonus programs to be effective the individual must know exactly what he or she needs to do to receive the bonus. Traditional lump-sum bonuses, based on management's goodwill and usually handed out at Christmas, bear no relationship to productivity because such bonuses are given at a fixed time, not after a period of successful performance.

6. Pay for skills

A recent trend is to increase compensation as employees increase their skill levels. The assumption is that multiskilled workers add more value in the new team-oriented environment. Increased skills also make it possible to use job rotation as a means of motivating employees.

The various efforts undertaken over the last few decades to give employees something more than the basic wage reflect widespread dissatisfaction with the existing compensation model, and a recognition that it is ineffective. These efforts have prepared the way for a new model that gives each individual a genuine stake in the success of the business. The broad outline of the new model is provided on the following pages.

Key Point: There is no magic formula. Any plan that places greater incentives among the work force will produce a net return above the dilution created. If the company or institution is willing to give a little, they will get a great deal in return.

THE RAPIDRESPONSE COMPENSATION MODEL

The RapidResponse enterprise requires a new compensation approach, one that can transform the "people side" of the company. The new compensation system is anchored in the business goals. Creating linkage between compensation and business goals requires a redesign of both base pay and of programs that provide variable incentives. There is no "one size fits all" when it comes to redesigning compensation systems to promote employee commitment. However, there are some general principles that should be kept in mind. Here the discussion of the new RapidResponse compensation paradigm is divided into two parts:

1. The redesign of base pay
2. The design of variable compensation

Within the broad guidelines outlined next, each company has room to develop its own unique system for giving employees a stake in the success of the enterprise.

THE REDESIGN OF BASE PAY

In the RapidResponse enterprise base pay is no longer a nonvalue-added element of an entitlement system. Pay becomes an integral element of business strategy. This requires a process for designing compensation systems that align pay with the business objectives. The pay system is built directly and systematically on the business objectives and the requirements of the RapidResponse operating environment.

The new approach to pay involves reinforcing broad, flexible job descriptions. It encourages and rewards the development of a portfolio of skills that are needed in the new work environment.

The design of a new pay system will present a real challenge to those compensation specialists who have had a major investment in traditional systems. It is clear, as I have already indicated, that human resources professionals have a difficult time letting go of old practices. Some companies may need to go outside to get the expertise needed to redesign the pay system.

The introduction of a new approach to pay is also a challenge to employees. The typical promotion mind-set, with its "climb-the-ladder" mentality, reinforces a multilayered bureaucratic structure. As the hierarchy flattens, the opportunity for promotion will disappear. There is no magic potion for addressing this promotion mind-set. First, people will need to be reeducated to the realities of the workplace of the 1990s. They need to understand the changes taking place—a general shift from the promotion mind-set to a developing-my-skills-portfolio mind-set. Developing this skills portfolio involves lateral moves and the willingness and ability to learn. Climbing a bureaucratic ladder does not necessarily provide the broad learning experiences needed for effectiveness in the modern business environment.

The development of a new pay system, suitable for the RapidResponse environment, will require new policies that support developing a skills portfolio. The challenge, as the hierarchy disappears, is to create innovative and satisfying new career progressions.

DESIGN OF VARIABLE COMPENSATION

An effective program of variable incentives/rewards is a critical element in reinforcing the RapidResponse operating environment. The key is to create a strong and direct connection to the success of the enterprise. Important issues to consider when developing variable incentives are as follows:

1. *Involve employees during the design phase.* Creating a task force that has compensation expertise as well as broad employee rep-

resentation is an effective way to develop a system that gives each individual a stake in the success of the venture.

2. *Make it possible for employees to share in bottom-line results.* Employees will only develop a true sense of ownership for results if they have the opportunity to share in those results. The key idea is to create profits and then have owners, investors, management, and front-line employees all share in these gains. While some of the traditional incentive programs, such as the Scanlon Plan, focus on specific areas of performance, the RapidResponse model presented here allows everyone in a particular facility to share in the bottom line. Some progressive companies are now using a new benchmark for measuring performance known as *economic value added (EVA)*. EVA is defined as net operating profits after the company deducts a charge for all the capital it uses, including for plants, inventories, and accounts receivable. This objective system makes it possible to measure the performance of the entire company or of the individual business unit.

3. *The incentives must be capable of communicating a clear message to employees.* Participants must understand that they do indeed have a real stake in the success of the company. The company must be willing to put real money on the table. Gimmicky programs that give nickle-and-dime results will not build worker commitment. These programs may gain some short-term public relations benefits, but they do not communicate the message that people have an investment in the success of the enterprise.

4. *Management must believe that workers hold the key to success in the marketplace.* The willingness to put real money on the table requires a shift in mind-set by the people at the top. At some level, owners and executives must come to understand that workers are entitled to a fair share of the benefits derived from their labor. This shift in thinking will be difficult for many who have deeply ingrained traditional beliefs about the rights of workers. The development of the new RapidResponse approach to compensation is based on a win-win mind-set. Too few executives understand that the new approach to compensation will not merely contribute to increased loyalty and commitment, but

will also result in an increase in return on investment for the owners and investors.

5. *Implementing a new compensation system requires strong leadership.* Any change in the status quo is likely to encounter resistance. Workers in general and unions in particular have a deep distrust of management when it comes to matters of compensation. The long history of adversarial relationships between workers and management has left workers suspicious of profit-sharing initiatives. What is required is leadership at the top that has the trust and confidence of the work force. This issue of leadership will be explored more fully in Chapter Eight. Clearly, unless managers become convinced that higher levels of commitment are essential for success, they are not likely to change old attitudes.

6. *Creating a new compensation system requires a new vision of how the workplace should operate.* Historically, management has had a "give-them-as-little-as-possible" attitude. Managers were recognized for their ability to negotiate tough deals with the labor unions. The issue of compensation contributed toward the creation of a two-class system in which workers feel they have little investment in the company. In many ways, compensation has become a wasted investment, with the company gaining little commitment for the money expended. Developing a compensation system that gives employees a stake in the success of the enterprise requires replacing the adversarial relationship with a *partnership* based on mutual interest.

Case Study:
Cin-Made Corporation

When Robert Frey and his partner purchased Cin-Made Corporation in 1984, they faced a tough challenge. A small Cincinnati-based company, Cin-Made manufactured mailing tubes and composite cans. It was a troubled company with marginal profits, out-of-control labor costs, rigid job descriptions, and very poor labor relations. Frey has told the story of how he transformed this 90-year-old company into a high-performance, highly profitable enterprise in "Empowerment or Else," a *Harvard Business Review* article (September-October 1993). Giving employees a stake in the success of the business was a major factor in the transformation. In a recent conversation with Mr. Frey, he explained that his original *HBR* article had *underestimated* the true benefits of his plan for the company and for the employees.

Frey describes candidly the adversarial relationship that had existed between management and the workers during the years after he became an owner. It was clear that Frey, as a hard-nosed businessman, was on a collision course with his employees and that the results could be detrimental to both sides. Somewhere along the way he began to understand the need to create a new dynamic in the workplace. In the *HBR* article he writes, "What the company needed was an atmosphere of teamwork and participation, whereas the atmosphere we had was adversarial and acrimonious. Acrimonious because we had short tempers and big egos. Adversarial because management and labor have always been adversaries. Unions were created to be adversarial. Adversarial was what my training and experience as a manager had prepared me for."

Frey initiated monthly state-of-the-business meetings to give employees a better understanding of the business. He began studying profit-sharing plans. His idea was to create a tangible connection between the way people worked and the profits they shared. This is how he described his approach: "I wanted to do something radical. I wanted to divide employee income into fixed and variable components. I wanted to make profit-sharing—the variable component—so big that is would serve as an incentive to keep wages—the fixed component—frozen." The plan he adopted called for giving 35% of before-tax profits to managers and workers. Hourly workers would get equal shares of 18% of profits, apportioned by hours worked (except overtime). Managers and office staff would divide another 17% on the basis of performance appraisals.

Frey had to overcome initial resistance from both managers and workers. However, the substantial profit-sharing checks, given out three times a year, had a major impact on morale and performance. Robert Frey, in describing the results, makes an eloquent argument for giving employees a stake in the company's success: "The effect has been electrifying. Full-time employees now routinely monitor the work of temps to reduce waste and increase efficiency. Strict adherence to job descriptions is a thing of the past. Absenteeism has fallen to nearly nil. Productivity is up 30%. Grievances are down to one or two a year. Except for skill-based pay, there has been no increase in fixed wages since 1984, yet our work force makes more money than comparable industrial workers . . . today I discover to my surprise that whereas once I pushed them forward, now they are pushing me."

FOUR LESSONS FROM EXPERIENCE

The following practical suggestions for introducing profit sharing are based on the experiences of DGI consultants.

1. *Include all levels.* The goal is to get the entire organization pulling together synergistically so that everybody can win. However, the system can be designed in such a way as to make allowances for individuals who shoulder additional responsibilities.

2. *Tie bonuses to bottom-line results.* The real measure of success for any company is reflected in the financials. Delivering a more effective just-in-time program is of little value if the company is losing out in the marketplace. One of the keys to building a RapidResponse work environment is getting everyone concerned about the bottom line. Of course the investment by employees in the bottom line must be accompanied by the sharing of business information as described in Chapter Four.

3. *Use the incentive plan to reinforce performance.* We know from behavioral science that a payment received on an annual basis has very little reinforcement value. Bonus payments made on a quarterly or more frequent basis are more effective in building employee commitment than end-of-year lump-sum payments.

4. *Communicate honestly with employees.* Open-book management is a requirement for profit sharing. Withholding information only increases distrust on the part of employees.

"BEGIN WITH THE END IN MIND"

To sum up, variable compensation can be a powerful motivator. Companies that have embraced this concept have been on a growth trajectory. Smart managers have begun to realize that there must be a direct sharing of the gains to achieve the high levels of employee commitment needed in a tough, turbulent marketplace.

The admonition to "begin with the end in mind," in Steven Covey's *Seven Habits of Highly Effective People*, is appropriate when it comes to changing current compensation practices. The business leader who sets out to build a RapidResponse organization, including a new compensation system, needs to understand where the effort is leading. One of the themes of this book is that the new high-performance enterprise cannot be built without a new set of management assumptions. The most difficult of these assumptions has to do with the way that employees are compensated for their work. The reluctance of management to embrace profit sharing is understandable: The old assumptions have rarely been questioned, even in progressive MBA programs. The widely accepted view is that pay is an entitlement rather than a means of engaging the work force in a partnership to achieve mutually beneficial results. And except for commissioned salespeople, most employees can do little to influence the amount of compensation received. Bringing about a change will require a *cultural transformation*. This means that certain *attitudes* will have to change. The strategies that can be used to change old attitudes will be the major focus of attention in Chapters Ten and Eleven.

The need to change the compensation system in traditionally managed companies is an issue that has been largely ignored by the gurus of the management consulting field. Books on total quality management and business reengineering rarely address compensation as a consideration in building a successful business. The authors of these books ignore the critical role that compensation plays in building the high-performance, market-responsive enterprise.

THE CHALLENGE: SELLING RAPIDRESPONSE CONCEPTS

We have devoted one chapter to each of the three core principles that constitute RapidResponse management, the goal being to provide some concrete suggestions on how the principles can be implemented. However, there is a lot of room for experimentation. Managers need to know that implementation is much more difficult and complex than might appear on the surface. One of the recurring themes of this book is that the three core assumptions of RapidResponse management can only be integrated into an existing organization by means of a change in company culture. As will be explained in later chapters, there is an important psychological dimension involved in getting employees to change their attitudes, beliefs, and patterns of behavior. Understanding what the three secrets of RapidResponse management are is only a first step. *Selling these concepts to the entire work force is the foremost challenge facing company management.* Perhaps the single most important element in moving through the cultural barriers has to do with having "the end in sight." The need to have a compelling *vision*, capable of pulling the organization forward, is discussed in the next chapter.

Creating the Resilient Organization: Lesson 6

The resilient organization of the future will have employees who are truly *committed* to the success of the enterprise. This commitment comes from a sense of personal investment in the success of the company. We refer to this sharing of ownership as the third secret of RapidResponse management. It is one of the foundations on which to build tomorrow's resilient organization.

CHAPTER 7

TRANSFORMING YOUR ORGANIZATION:
Begin with a Vision for the Future

"This *vision* stuff is not going to add to the bottom line." These words, spoken by a hard-nosed businessman, reflect a widely shared view of the visioning process among executives and managers. Ask any business leader what his or her vision is for the future of the company, and you are likely to get a quick summary of the strategic plan. Nevertheless, a clear motivating vision, one that defines the future direction of the company, can serve as a powerful magnet to pull the organization forward. Indeed, creating a practical vision that can be clearly communicated to the work force is an absolute requirement for building a high-performance organization.

Unfortunately, the word *vision* has been overused and has lost much of its power and meaning. Several years ago George Bush earned himself considerable ridicule for his reference to the "vision thing." Bush was really reflecting a skepticism about visioning that is pervasive in the business community. Vision is up there with "team building" and "communication" as part of the soft side of management. In reality, the concept often seems vague and nebulous. The word carries negative connotations because it has come to signify wishful thinking rather than business reality. The use of trendy vision statements with phrases like "becoming number one" or "achieving world-class status" have tended to devalue the concept. These statements, displayed prominently, often reflect nothing more than an effort to convince others about how good they are. Some of these so-called "vision" statements are taken directly from the pages of popular management books. The empty-sounding rhetoric is not likely to have impact on the day-to-day performance of employees.

VISION SHOULD DRIVE *PERFORMANCE*

A vision statement is a conceptual road map that shows people in the organization where they are going. It serves as a bridge between the present and the future. In most organizations today, people experience history and tradition as powerful influences pulling them *backward*. A clear, practical vision should have the power to pull people *forward*. The value of the vision statement is that it provides the leverage need-ed to the organization to let go of the past.

People sometimes confuse the concept of vision with *mission*. A mission statement simply states the rationale for the existence of the organization—to provide certain goods or services to a particular seg-ment of the market. For example, the mission statement of an acute care city hospital might be to provide emergency services to low-income residents of the community. The vision statement, on the other hand, is the deepest expression of what the organization wants to become. The vision statement for a bank might be to become known in the business community as the financial institution that provides the most personalized service. The future becomes the cause of current behavior. Clearly, for the vision to be effective, it must have *emotional appeal* for the people who work in the organization. Very often the vision will call on people to make personal changes in atti-tudes and behaviors. We know enough about the psychodynamics of change to know that these personal changes are not easy. The vision must be powerful enough for people to want to take risks and make painful changes.

The vision statement is the deepest expression of what the organization wants to become.

VISION AS A MOTIVATOR

The vision must create a mental picture of a future state that is more attractive than the present, thereby challenging people to greatness. A vision for the future that is properly communicated throughout the organization provides a basis for getting everyone aligned in the same direction. In Figure 7.1, the large arrow represents the whole organization. The smaller arrows within the larger arrow represent individuals and groups. This diagram shows an organization in which *everyone* is aligned in pursuit of a common vision for the future. This would be a very rare occurrence! In most business organizations the arrows point in all directions. There is no clearly shared sense of direction or common purpose. Ask employees and managers where the organization is heading and you will get a hodge-podge of answers. This lack of vision seriously hampers the ability of the organization to move forward. Clearly, when the resources within an organization are aligned in the same direction, there are few limitations as to what can be accomplished. Vision allows people to be connected together synergistically. Some of the best examples of people aligned in pursuit of a vision are found in professional sports.

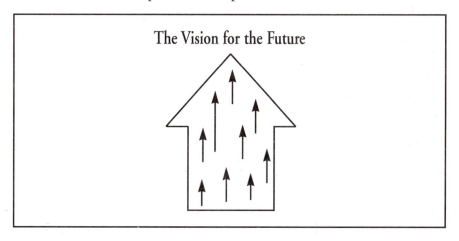

Figure 7.1.
Arrows indicate organizational alignment.

Executives and managers often have difficulty with the concept of vision because they are more accustomed to "left-brain" activity; that is, they like to deal with specific quantifiable goals. The idea of engaging in a creative process, of using the right brain, to create a mental picture of a desirable future state, is something outside their comfort zone. Creating a vision for the future of the business is not a mechanistic process similar to that used in developing a strategic plan. When the management of an organization comes together to create a future vision of greatness they ask the question: *What do we want to become?* The answer to this question always involves a certain amount of right-brain activity. However, the formulation of that vision is not the result of some sudden inspiration. The leaders look *within* the organization at its resources and look *outside* at the opportunities in deciding on a direction for the future. It is not uncommon for management to go off-site for a few days to work on creating a vision for the future, as such creative activity cannot be successfully undertaken in an environment where there are interruptions.

FORMULATING A VISION: PRACTICAL GUIDELINES

Developing a clear statement on where the company wants to go might seem to be a simple activity. However, many companies develop statements that have little motivational power. Here are four guidelines for managers engaged in the visioning process:

1. *Avoid cliches, slogans, and jargon.* Terms such as "excellence" and "world class" have lost their meaning from overuse.

2. *Make it comprehensible to every employee.* Keep in mind that a significant percentage of workers are functionally illiterate. Can people on the loading dock communicate the vision? What about maintenance staff? The most effective vision statements appeal to the competitive instincts of *all* employees. A good vision statement will conjure up a mental picture. In a recent speech, Bill Gates described the vision for Microsoft Corporation as "putting information at the fingertips of everyone."

3. *Include statements that will challenge/stretch employees.* The problem with many vision statements is that they ask *too little* of stakeholders.

4. Use the vision statement as a "soundbite" to signal *future directions.* A well-crafted statement can serve as a rallying cry for the entire organization.

VISION SETS THE *DIRECTION*

The vision for the future allows management to *position* the organization for success. Clearly, it is not enough to simply state where they want the organization to be in the next two or three years. Rather, the organization must be pointed in the right overall direction. Marketing managers have long been familiar with the notion of product positioning. For example, an automobile company, in bringing a new car to market, would need to decide in what niche it would compete. It could be a high-performance model, competing against BMW or Porsche. Or it could be expensive and conservative, competing against Mercedes and Cadillac. Alternatively, it could be competing in a less expensive niche that included Chevrolets. This basic concept can be extended to organizational positioning. Organizational positioning refers to the process by which the organization designs, establishes, and sustains a viable niche in the external environment. Part of establishing a vision of the future involves making decisions about how to position the business in the external environment.

A NEED FOR *CONTINUOUS* POSITIONING

In the new business environment change can occur with lightning speed. As a result, nothing is more important to modern organizations than their effectiveness in coping with change. The organization must have the ability to quickly *reposition* itself in response to a continuously changing marketplace. In the old days management could develop a five-year plan and sit back and monitor implementation of the plan. Today, that would be a recipe for certain failure.

RapidResponse management provides the organization with the agility and flexibility to make *quick* navigational adjustments. In other words, with RapidResponse management it becomes possible to quickly make navigational adjustments as the need arises.

The organization must have the ability to quickly reposition itself in response to a continuously changing marketplace.

In tomorrow's business environment, management will need to be engaged in a process of *continuous positioning.* Of course it is not enough just to point the business in the right direction; the organization itself must have the flexibility to take advantage of new and unexpected opportunities. The business landscape is covered with the remains of companies that were unable to see the changes that were coming or were unable to make needed strategic adjustments. Companies like Wang and Prime Computer are examples of businesses that failed to reposition themselves in response to market changes. Unfortunately, a recognition of the need for repositioning is not enough. An increasing number of executives are discovering that their organizations are hampered by cumbersome bureaucracy and an apathetic work force that prevent making needed adjustments.

Market strategy setting, an integral part of positioning, is based on both the markets and on competitors' capabilities. Setting a marketing strategy involves broad-based decisions regarding the market positions to which the company and its products should aspire. The process starts with the broad vision that is then translated into a very concrete marketing strategy. It is a dynamic process that allows management to continuously respond to changing market conditions.

A key question for business leaders to ask in setting market strategy is: *Where do we concentrate our energies and resources?* No company can be "all things to all people." The concentration decision involves examining market wants and needs, and what the competitor does and doesn't do, and then deciding on a niche where you can successfully compete. Positioning provides the context for the market strategy. Once market strategy has been set, leaders must continue to ask themselves regularly: *What business are we in?*

The vision describes a desirable and achievable future state. This leads to a process whereby the business is positioned in the marketplace, all the while maintaining the ability to respond quickly. *The process of building the RapidResponse organization of the future begins with the visioning and positioning as described in this chapter.* This is not an esoteric or abstract process: The ability to reposition *quickly* in response to changing conditions has become a condition for survival. The company of tomorrow will be able to make the correct concentration decision and be in a position to act on new possibilities.

VISION AS THE FOUNDATION FOR *RAPIDRESPONSE* MANAGEMENT

Creating a vision represents a necessary and indispensable first step in the process of building a high-performance enterprise. It provides the context for introducing the three core concepts of RapidResponse management to members of the organization. It is much easier to give employees information on "the business of the business" if management has a clear sense of direction. Similarly, the process of identifying and redesigning key business processes becomes much easier when the future direction has been established. Finally, a clear practical vision provides the basis for developing a compensation system whereby employees will know that they are entrepreneurs working for themselves as well as for the corporation.

The relationship of vision, positioning, and RapidResponse management is illustrated in Figure 7.2.

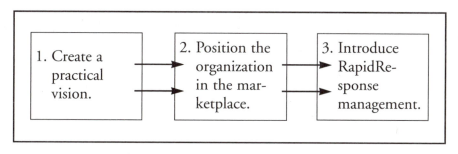

Figure 7.2.
The path to success in the new busines environment.

It is clear from Figure 7.2 that creating a high-performance organization involves more than introducing a new set of operating principles. RapidResponse management is a means toward an end. To paraphrase Steven Covey's admonition: The process of integrating RapidResponse management practices begins with the vision in mind. The radical streamlining of work processes and the building of worker commitment can come about only when everyone is heading in the same direction. Figure 7.2 shows the process of building the high-performance organization as involving three critical steps:

Step 1. Create a practical *vision.*

Step 2. *Position* the business in the marketplace.

Step 3. Introduce *RapidResponse* concepts.

An organization without vision will not survive for long in a marketplace that is chaotic and constantly changing. It is not just a question of working hard or producing a quality product or service: The company must also find the right market niche. In addition to articulating a vision of a desired future state, the *internal resources* of the organization must be organized in such a way as to respond to opportunities.

The three enterprises discussed in Chapter Two were led by individuals who had a good sense of the direction in which their respective organizations should be heading. One of their challenges was to communicate their vision to the people around them. An equally important task was to get positioned in the marketplace to take advantage of changing conditions. Finally, each of these leaders faced the challenge of making the organization itself responsive to the new opportunities.

SETTING THE DIRECTION:
A WORKSHOP FOR MANAGEMENT

One of the characteristics of our Western civilization is the tendency to want to reduce every challenge to a set of logical steps. Much of the attraction of total quality management and business process reengineering for executives and managers is that they offer a step-by-step formula for changing organizations. Executives with technical backgrounds, such as engineers, respond favorably to this mechanistic approach to managing change. The human side of enterprise gets ignored. Unfortunately, these approaches will continue to be popular, even if the evidence of success is missing, as they speak to the needs of business leaders who hold mechanistic views of change management.

Recognizing the need for the people at the top to have an opportunity for visioning, the DGI Group developed a workshop called *A Gathering of Leaders*. This two-day workshop is designed to engage senior managers in the creative process of setting a direction for the company. Similar programs have been developed by other consulting groups. The workshop provides an opportunity for the people at the top to engage in the right-brain activity needed in creating a future vision and in positioning the organization in the external environment. While the structure of these sessions will vary depending on the unique needs of the group, the workshop is designed to encourage as much creative thinking as possible.

The first step involves fostering synergy and increasing communication among the managers who are participating. In some instances a psychological assessment instrument is completed prior to the session to help increase mutual understanding between members. The primary goal at the beginning of the workshop is to create a high level of trust and open communication. For some management groups it is more effective to involve them in some form of physical activity such as white-water rafting. These activities should be facilitated by an individual who understands the corporate environment and who has a solid background in the behavioral sciences.

While there is a tendency to refer to the group of managers at the top of an organization as the "management team," the reality is that this group rarely functions as a team. The goal in the *Gathering of Leaders Workshop* is to build on the valuable differences that exist between members of the group. The workshop is designed in such as way as to allow the managers to "clear their heads" before beginning work on the creative process involved in creating a vision for the future.

Putting Psychology to Work

The use of psychology in the workplace is looked upon with skepticism by many managers. It falls into the category of "soft stuff." Some of the negativity goes back to the 1960s and 1970s, when off-site retreats, using sensitivity techniques, were in vogue. These sessions were often facilitated by individuals who lacked the experience and skills needed to handle an outpouring of intense feelings. The general ambivalence of managers toward psychology carries over to their attitude toward psychological assessment instruments. Often, managers also have legitimate concerns about the invasion of privacy.

Because of the concerns of management, companies miss out on the use of highly effective psychological tools. For example, the *Myers-Briggs Type Indicator* can be used to greatly enhance communication between members of any work group. In Chapter Thirteen I will show how an instrument known as the *style analysis* can be used as a tool to help create a RapidResponse work environment.

While psychological tests can be misused, management should consider their value as they seek to identify people who will support the changes they are introducing.

To get the creative juices flowing, members engage in a free-wheeling discussion of the future of the business. The first question is simply: *What do we want to become?* Other questions that can be asked are:

- What is it that we have to offer the world?
- What are our unique strengths and capabilities?
- What changes will happen in the next two or three years that could have a major effect on our business?
- What are the strengths and weaknesses of our competitors?

These questions are not designed to produce a strategic plan but to develop a picture of the business in the future that is at once attractive, challenging, and successful. The task of reducing that vision of the future to one comprehensible statement is not easy and will usually require many hours of intense discussion. The statement must resonate with people at every level.

Once the vision of the future has been formulated, the group explores how they can position the business in the external environment. They look at what is going on *within* the organization and what they see happening on the *outside*. The matching up of the internal resources with emerging opportunities in the marketplace contributes toward the development of an understanding of future opportunities.

Managers leave the two-day *Gathering of Leaders Workshop* with a clear sense of where they want to lead the company. The workshop can also be incorporated into a five-stage change process known as the *blitz change strategy*. A detailed discussion of this model, poineered by Deevy Gilligan International, is provided in Chapter Ten.

THE REAL TEST: WILL PEOPLE SIGN ON?

When management clarify the vision and set a direction, they have completed only about 50% of the task. After they return from the off-site workshop they are confronted with an equally important task: how to get *every employee* signed on. A recurring theme in this book is that traditional work organizations must undergo *revolutionary* change to respond successfully to a continuously changing business environment. This requires a new vision of what the organization can become. *Employees must share in that vision if they are to be committed to its fulfillment.* Several years ago we started using the words "rapid response" to describe the essential nature of this new organizational form. When the leaders return from the workshop, they are often confronted with the need to change the culture of the organization that they left behind. The extent to which the organization will need to be reinvented will vary from one organization to another. The *RapidResponse Readiness Checklist*, found at the end of this book, provides management with a guide to measuring the amount of internal work that will need to be undertaken. The formulation of a clear and powerful vision statement will provide the leverage needed for pulling the organization out of its comfort zone.

In summary, management must set the direction and then communicate it to the entire work force. The vision by itself will accomplish nothing. In fact, it can become an object of ridicule if not properly sold to employees. A legitimate vision, engraved in the consciousness of every employee, is the foundation for building the winning organization of the future.

Creating the Resilient Organization:
Lesson 7

In a turbulent environment, employees need to be able to "see light at the end of the tunnel." Employees must also find meaning in their work. The organization must have a sense of direction. Creating a practical vision for the future is an essential step in setting the direction and in giving people a reason for wanting to come to work. The resilient organization has the ability to cope with adversity because it has a sense of its own future.

CHAPTER 8

THE LEADER WHO IS TRUSTED:
A Core Requirement

Are business executives the most demanding and egotistical individuals in society? In conducting psychological assessments on over 500 senior level managers, using an instrument called *Managing for Success*, I discovered that an overwhelming majority were at the top of the dominance scale. Thus, the image of the CEO as a hard-driving individual willing to do whatever it takes to maximize profits seems to be accurate.

Hard-driving business leaders often have little patience with what they perceive as the "soft" side of management. Concepts like "empowerment" and "ownership" are meaningless to them. Indeed, CEOs like Lee Iacocca and "neutron" Jack Welch are respected and feared exactly because they take a "slash and burn" approach to management. Interestingly, research conducted by Deevy Gilligan International shows that while such executives are frequently perceived by subordinates as intimidating and coercive, they perceive themselves as practitioners of participatory management.

Many managers at the middle and upper levels have learned to master the statistical and mechanical tools they need to make their organizations competitive. What they don't understand is that these tools are only part of the story. Here it is useful to distinguish between *management* and *leadership*. Management has to do with analyzing a specific problem and developing a sequence of actions to deal with it. Good management implies *doing things the right way*. Leadership, on the other hand, has to do with *doing the right things*. In the traditionally managed organization there is often an abundance of management and very little leadership.

Many companies try to *manage* change. However, old-line management, which teaches managers to plan, organize, lead, and control, has little to do with creating a high-performance work environment. RapidResponse management requires more than incremental changes in the way things are done on a day-to-day basis. Getting people to embrace and seek a vision that requires them to break through familiar ways of thinking and acting demands strong personal leadership from the people at the top.

Building the new RapidResponse work environment will require a set of attitudes, beliefs, and behaviors that many business leaders, schooled in the traditional command-and-control style, will find difficult to accept. In fact, the task of changing a mature company into a RapidResponse enterprise requires leadership attributes that are in scarce supply.

Leadership is defined as the ability to influence the behavior of others. A fundamental requirement of authentic leadership is that the leader have *a basic belief in the potential of people*. Related to his or her belief in people, the leader must *be perceived by the work force as someone who is trustworthy*. There is overwhelming evidence that the executive who has a low opinion of people or who sees employees as expendable will not command respect or loyalty. People are simply not inspired by a leader who does not see their potential for greatness, nor are they willing to make a genuine emotional commitment to a leader who is less than trustworthy.

THE LEADER MUST RECOGNIZE THE TRUE POTENTIAL OF PEOPLE

Leadership in a corporate sense is the ability to bridge the gap between the organization's goals on the one hand and its capabilities on the other. Being a leader means being a catalyst, an enabler. It means bringing out the best in people. The effective leader creates an environment where people can learn and grow. It begins with what the leader's view of people is. The truly inspiring leader is able to persuade people to do more than they believe they can. The successful organization is one in which *ordinary* people accomplish extraordinary things.

Despite popular perceptions, the effective leader is not someone who persuades employees to do something through charismatic personality traits. The leader believes in people. Leadership comes from *within*. Ultimately, leadership has less to do with who's "in charge" and more to do with individual strengths and convictions.

One of the unfortunate legacies of the traditional hierarchical organization is that workers at lower levels are often devalued. In focus groups and interviews, the refrain is familiar: "I don't get respect." The true potential of employees goes unrecognized. The difference between the people at the bottom and the people who manage the organization usually has more to do with educational opportunities and official credentials than with natural intelligence; almost every organization has people at the bottom who are as smart as the people at the top.

Case Study: Recognizing *Hidden* Potential

The following story, which first appeared on the pages of *The New York Times* on September 10, 1989, illustrates the unrecognized potential of employees. The story, as told by Max Depree, the CEO of Herman Miller, was excerpted from a remarkable little book, *Leadership Is an Art* (New York: Dell, 1989). Depree and his family have created one of the most admired and successful companies in the

United States. They know from personal experience that the true potential of employees can go unrecognized:

"My father is ninety-six years old. He is the founder of Herman Miller, and much of the impounded energy of the company, a legacy still drawn on today, is part of his contribution. In the furniture business of the 1920's the machines of most factories were not run by electric motors, but by pulleys from a central drive shaft. The central drive shaft was run by the steam engine. The steam engine got its steam from the boiler. The boiler, in our case, got its fuel from the sawdust and other waste coming out of the machine—a beautiful cycle.

"The millwright was the person who oversaw that cycle and on whom the entire activity of the operation depended. He was a key person.

One day the millwright died.

"My father, being a young manager at the time, did not particularly know what he should do when a key person died, but thought he ought to visit the family. He went to the house and was invited to join the family in the living room. There was some awkward conversation—the kind with which many of us are familiar.

"The widow asked my father if it would be all right if she read aloud some poetry. Naturally, he agreed. She went into another room, came back with a bound book, and for many minutes read selected pieces of beautiful poetry. When she finished, my father commented on how beautiful the poetry was and asked who wrote it. She replied that her husband, the millwright, was the poet."

A belief in the potential of all people is a requirement for the leader of the RapidResponse enterprise. This means letting go Theory X stereotypes that label workers as intrinsically lazy and unmotivated. In work with all kinds of organizations I have been constantly reminded of how frequently the true potential of workers goes unrecognized. *The story of the millwright highlights an important fact:*

Creativity can be found at every level, irrespective of academic credentials or job title. The manager who fails to see true potential will not motivate employees to stretch themselves.

Pat Riley, coach of the New York Knicks, is a model of the kind of leadership needed in building a high-performance organization. He helped transform a mediocre professional basketball team into world-class competitors simply by helping them realize their true potential. The secret of Riley's success has been his ability to communicate to the players his belief in their ability to be the best in the National Basketball League.

The leader in the RapidResponse enterprise creates a work environment where people are encouraged to contribute according to their true potential. The leader gives lower-level employees meaningful information on company finances. He or she provides opportunities to pursue entrepreneurial activity. The people who are closest to the work are allowed to make decisions about process improvements. There is recognition that people at lower levels are generally better at recognizing opportunities for process simplification.

A genuine belief in the hidden potential of people is the basis for promoting employee involvement. While the concept of worker participation is glibly discussed in newspapers and magazines, "empowerment" programs are often nothing more than superficial efforts to make employees *feel* involved. And while a growing number of companies refer to employees as "partners" or "associates," these terms do little more than create the illusion of participation. Real worker empowerment grows out of a conviction about the gifts that employees bring to the workplace. Although few workers have the poetic talent of the millwright, they typically have more to offer than is recognized.

THE LEADER MUST BE TRUSTWORTHY

Business leaders, in addition to recognizing the true potential of employees, must also be seen as trustworthy. The need for the leader to be trusted is rarely discussed in textbooks on management. Somehow the concept of trustworthiness is not associated with strong effective leadership. Nevertheless, it is obvious that the executive who loses credibility will not be effective: employees have a "sixth sense" that tells them when the leader is not credible. To paraphrase the title of a recently published book on leadership: you've got to be believed to be heard.

Trust is the basic fabric that holds an organization together. If we can't trust the boss, if we can't trust the management of the company, then we have nothing on which to build a truly collaborative effort.

The majority of people still believe that an organization can be rationally designed and that rational design will overcome the chaotic world we live in. Baloney. Seventy percent of the problem is trust and faith and human decency and character. All of our formal university, college and corporate training ignores the 70% and teaches the 30%, the rational part.

Peter Vaill,
quoted in *OD Practitioner* (Spring 1993)

Trust is not some abstract concept. It is the cement that builds relationships. We need trust in every aspect of our lives, including our relationships in the workplace. There has been, however, a deep fundamental change in the way we view the world today, and as a result, trust is no longer fashionable. Employees who once believed in devoting their entire working lives to one organization have seen so many colleagues tossed out in the restructurings of the 1980s that they become emotionally uninvolved in their jobs. In fact, according to *Industry Week* (July 17, 1989), workers simply don't trust management. While 87% of the workers polled think it is very important that "management is honest, upright, and ethical," only 39% believe that it is. That is a major change from one generation ago when workers implicitly trusted managers. Each new "restructuring," accompanied by well-crafted press releases, adds to the cynicism that already pervades the workplace.

If businesses are to thrive and to regain competitiveness, trust must be more than something that is talked about. Organizations cannot be jungles where only the fittest survive. If companies are to motivate employees and to win their loyalty, they must change the way relationships are constructed. This rebuilding must begin with a leader who demonstrates integrity in the way he or she deals with people who work for their organizations.

"Drive out fear" was the cryptic advice of quality guru Edwards Deming. Workers will not be committed to coming up with creative and innovative solutions to problems in an environment characterized by fear and distrust. Defensiveness and mutual suspicion are antithetical to creating a highly productive environment. Obviously, trust is not something that can be built in an instant. It is earned by actions repeated over time. It begins with the people at the top.

When the CEO says that "there will be no more layoffs" and then, a few days later, authorizes staff reductions, trust goes out the window. Similarly, when the person at the top says that "quality is the number one commitment," and then allows defective parts to be shipped, credibility suffers. To build a high-performance organization, *employees must see the leader as someone who can be trusted.* There is an old cliché that suggests that recovering lost trust may be as difficult as trying to regain lost virginity. Once trust is lost, the effectiveness of the leader is permanently diminished.

> *Candor is a way to treat people with dignity. You go out there and answer questions as directly as you can. Sometimes it's difficult, but it earns you credibility.*
>
> Lawrence Bossidy,
> CEO, AlliedSignal

Executives who have the responsibility of getting an organization to make difficult changes must have the confidence and support of the work force. This is not to suggest that they have to play a "nice guy" role. There is no conflict between being a very tough and determined leader and maintaining the trust and respect of employees. Further, a passionate commitment to change and the ability to stay the course are essential characteristics of the change agent.

As I have explained, the relationship between the corporation and the worker has been characterized by suspicion and distrust since the days of the industrial revolution. The challenge is to rebuild trust and confidence and to create a positive work climate. No gimmicks can accomplish this task: *The leader must be seen as someone who can be trusted.*

THE LEADER COMMUNICATES A VISION OF THE FUTURE

There is a prevailing view that businesses can somehow *manage their way to success.* I believe that the ability to lead, rather than the ability to manage, is critical in enabling a bureaucratic organization to move through a transformation process. Clearly, one of the most important responsibilities of the leader is to create a clear sense of direction, to present the organization with a vision of what it can become. Too many executives are so preoccupied with micromanaging that they do not have time to deal with creating the vision and setting the direction; they consider taking a group of top people off-site to consider future directions a waste of time.

The most effective leader is the individual who has the ability to articulate the vision to the work force in a way that gets people excited and motivated. The visionary leader points the way to the future in a way that inspires confidence and trust in his or her followers. Sometimes the leader will use a metaphor or an earthy expression to communicate his or her vision for the future.

THE LEADER NEEDS TO BE A PIONEER

It is easy for executives to lose sight of the big picture when they become preoccupied with microissues, but leadership is not about introducing change through mechanistics. Creating a RapidResponse environment requires *pioneering* leadership that enables employees to see beyond the present into the future.

The concept of the leader as a *pioneer* is very appropriate in a constantly evolving business environment: People at the top must see the possibilities to inspire others to follow them to the future.

Visionary leadership is a requirement for creating a high-performance enterprise.

Pioneers are willing to make an investment in the *human dynamics* side of change. They understand that this investment will determine their success in the 1990s and beyond, and they know that meaningful change requires a sustained effort over several years. They are not looking for some off-the-shelf program or motivational guru. As visionaries, they focus on the future and understand the need to bring moral authority to the task of leadership.

Unlike the traditional models of executive leadership, pioneers are not preoccupied with the use of power and authority: They are willing to abandon the *control* paradigm in favor of a work environment that values *commitment*. Employees are seen as "internal customers" who at various times will need support and direction. Creating a work environment that favors autonomy over dependence is the top priority.

THE LEADER CALLS THE "BIG PLAYS"

In searching for a way to describe the emerging role of management in the high-performance organization, a number of authors have used the analogy of the football team. In football, offensive and defensive coordinators manage the "process" of either moving the football down the field or keeping the opposition from doing so. Position coaches make sure pieces of the process are operating smoothly. The head coach—like any good leader—creates an environment in which people are inspired. In the RapidResponse enterprise the leader, like the effective head coach, doesn't tell people what to do or how to do it. He or she makes people *want* to contribute to the success of the enterprise in the marketplace. Like the head coach, the business leader is not preoccupied with day-to-day details. The leader focuses on the broader goals of helping the organization lose weight, become flexible, and stay hopeful. Because leaders are not concerned with details, they can call the "big plays" when needed.

Leadership That Inspires

The stereotypic image of corporate leaders has been of individuals who "kick ass and take names." This is known as *heroic* leadership. However, the new work environment demands a different type of leadership. Some refer to the new approach as postheroic leadership or *servant leadership*. These leaders lead by example and exercise quiet influence. They don't carry a big stick as the following three examples illustrate:

Nellie Curtin: When Nellie assumed leadership of a religious community of women in the early 1980s, she faced major challenges. The community was undergoing cataclysmic changes. At the professional level, the women were wrestling with how to move from a traditional service role to one of empowering poor communities to advocate on their own behalf. While some members were very forward in their thinking, all felt the pull of a several-hundred-year-old tradition. Differences in philosophy were especially apparent in intense generational differences.

When Nellie brought together superiors from the various communities for the annual meeting, the result was not what she expected. There was intense anger. There were stress, pain, and anxiety. And there was a lot of hurt. This was the first time that I observed Nellie exercise leadership. I had been invited to make a presentation on situational leadership. What I saw was a quiet, determined, unshakable woman leading her community through a most difficult catharsis. Her ability to listen to all points of view won her respect from the "young rebels" as well as from the traditionalists. What was unspoken was her conviction that this group could resolve its own issues.

Reggie Lewis: Before his sudden death of a heart condition, Reggie was Captain of the legendary Boston Celtics basketball team. Like other Boston fans, I came to admire the quiet but determined leadership Reggie provided for the team. A soft-spoken young man, he led by his actions more than by his words. In the process he won enormous respect not merely from fellow-players but from the whole Boston community. His teammates openly wept at his passing. In his short career in Boston, this young Afro-American, who had grown up in a Baltimore ghetto, demonstrated extraordinary leadership qualities. In spite of unresolved controversy surrounding his death, Reggie is remembered for the leadership he provided on and off the basketball court.

Rosmary Check: I came to know Rosemary after she asked me to conduct an employee opinion survey at the small rural New Hampshire hospital where she was CEO. When Rosemary assumed the leadership role, hospital employee morale was low, and there was deep distrust of management. One of her predecessors had been accused of embezzling funds, and another had a reputation as a capricious and manipulative manager. Like Nellie Curtin, Rosemary earned the confidence of others by showing concern for subordinates. Her style of leadership was quiet and low profile. When she made the rounds of the hospital, she did more listening than talking. Gradually, a bond of trust was restored between employees and management. After several years in the role of administrator, Rosemary decided that a leader with a different style would be necessary to move the hospital to another level.

THE MARY ROBINSON
LEADERSHIP MODEL

Women are increasingly assuming leadership roles in business, industry, and government. Mary Robinson, president of the Republic of Ireland, exemplifies the leadership attributes needed in the new business environment.

A graduate of Harvard University, Ms. Robinson had a distinguished career in the legal profession before she assumed the office of president. Since becoming president her influence has been extraordinary. At a time when people are highly cynical of public figures, she has gained the trust and confidence of people from all segments of society. Many managers speak of having "open-door" management. Mary Robinson practices an open style of leadership that offers genuine accessibility. The question that people ask is not "Have you met the president?" but "How many times have you met the president?"

Mary Robinson has used her office to help people see beyond the things that divide them. Her visit to the Queen of England, unprecedented in modern history, revealed a person who is willing to exercise leadership in breaking old stereotypes. Her visit to Somalia and subsequent visit to the United Nations were instrumental in focusing the attention of the world on this starving country. She has gained international recognition for her advocacy on behalf of Third World countries.

Mary Robinson has a clear vision of what she wants to accomplish through her office and the ability to communicate this vision to others. When she speaks, people listen because they *believe* her. She has leadership qualities that might well be emulated in the business environment.

THE NORMAN SCHWARZKOPF MODEL

The merger and acquisition mania of the 1980s thrived on a "slash and burn" style of leadership that undermined employee loyalty and commitment. Employees at the middle and lower levels became extremely distrustful of top management. The fact that senior executives were given huge salary and bonus packages, even when companies were operating in red ink, did little to enhance the image of executive leadership. The role models of business leadership that emerged out of the 1980s are inadequate for creating a high-performance workplace.

A more appropriate role model for the kind of leadership needed in creating a RapidResponse environment is provided by General Norman Schwarzkopf, commander of the Allied troops during the Gulf War. Schwarzkopf was tough and demanding in pursuit of his objective. Like Robinson, Schwarzkopf had the ability to communicate a genuine concern for the people he was leading; he had the reputation as a general who had warm feelings for the troops. Creating a sense of community in pursuit of a goal was one of his major leadership priorities. General Schwarzkopf understood the value of having the trust and confidence of all the people under his command.

In the business community, as in war, what is needed is leaders who are tough, demanding and decisive in pursuit of strategic objectives. But this toughness must be combined with the ability to inspire the trust and confidence of people throughout the organization.

Creating the Resilient Organization:
Lesson 8

To survive and thrive in a turbulent environment requires leadership that has the trust and confidence of the work force. This leader, in addition to engendering trust and confidence, has the ability to recognize the true potential of employees at every level. Tomorrow's resilient organization will be led by an individual who inspires confidence and commitment.

CHAPTER 9

INTRODUCING THE NEW PARADIGM:

Get Middle Management to Buy In

For the past decade my colleagues and I in the DGI consulting group have been involved in supporting the introduction of new management practices in older established companies both in the United States and in Europe. In almost every instance, the single greatest challenge has been to generate middle management support for the new management practices.

My understanding of why middle-level managers can be so resistant to change was deepened as I became familiar with the ideas of Barry Oshry and his theories about the distribution of power in organizations. Oshry, a Boston-based management consultant, has developed a model that describes the roles of the three levels in a hierarchical organization. He describes how middle management, which he refers to as the "middles," are pulled in divergent directions and, as a consequence, feel vulnerable and weak.

What became clear to me is that a change strategy, designed to introduce RapidResponse management practices, must take into account the feelings of vulnerability on the part of department heads and supervisors. These managers can and will sabotage implementation if not given a chance to buy in. A strategy for introducing change that bypasses the "middles" will be doomed to failure.

OPEN SEASON ON MIDDLE MANAGERS

Historically, middle management have always experienced feelings of vulnerability. However, before the computer age they were considered a necessary link in the upward and downward flow of communication. In traditional hierarchical organizations they were needed to monitor the activities of people at the lower levels. In the command-and-control paradigm of management, the middle managers played a key role.

In the 1980s it became open season on middle managers. Over 3 million of these managers were down-sized, outplaced, and left wondering what had happened to job security. The "middles" have become particularly vulnerable as the business environment undergoes chaotic change. One 1992 American Management Association study reports that while middle managers were only about 5% of the work force at the companies it surveyed, they accounted for 22% of the layoffs. In growing numbers of companies, self-managed teams are taking over such standard supervisory duties as scheduling work, maintaining quality, and even administering pay and vacations. Meanwhile, the ever-expanding power and dwindling cost of computers have transformed information handling from a difficult, time-consuming job to a far easier and quicker one. In a very short time the role of the middle manager has been radically changed. However, in my view, the answer is not to have open season against the "middles." These managers have knowledge and experience that are vital to the success of the company. To be successful in the RapidResponse environment, however, these managers must undergo a process of reeducation.

THE PSYCHODYNAMICS OF CHANGE

What is overlooked in discussion of the changing role of middle managers is the individual psychodynamics involved. These managers are asked to let go of the old way of managing people and embrace a new role for which they have had no role models or training. Some executives naively believe that middle managers will change simply because they are told to change. The emotional and behavioral dimensions are often ignored. The contrast between old style management and the new approach is illustrated in Figure 9.1. This comparison between the old manager and the new manager highlights the amount of change that will be needed if middle managers are to be effective in the workplace of the future.

When we consider how difficult it is for any *individual* to change his or her behavior, it becomes clear that change within a *group* will only happen in a gradual manner. For example, an overweight person will not be able to make instant changes in behavioral patterns affecting the weight problem; clearly, the amount of time and degree of difficulty is compounded when a group of overweight persons are involved. The same psychological principles apply when a group of managers and supervisors need to make changes in attitudes and behavioral patterns. If the company has 45 managers, there will

Old Manager	*New* Manager
1. Thinks of self as a boss.	1. Thinks of self as a resource.
2. Follows a chain of command.	2. Networks with any individual or group to get the job done.
3. Needs a set organizational structure.	3. Works well in a fluid work environment.
4. Makes decisions alone.	4. Involves those who need to be involved.
5. Holds on to information.	5. Shares information.
6. Values long hours.	6. Values results.
7. Narrow skill base.	7. Broad portfolio of skills.

Figure 9.1.
The old manager versus the new manager.

be 45 individuals who will need to experience a change in behavior. Each of these individuals will respond in a unique way to the demands of the new business environment. However, it is fairly predictable that about one-third of this group will find it extremely difficult to make the needed changes.

Not all middle managers will be able to adapt to the new work environment. However, it is important that all be given *support* in this difficult process. Trained for the Machine Age, these managers are having to learn how to function in the Information Age. Executives tend to *overestimate* the ability of middle managers to make necessary changes.

THE MANAGER AS HERO

Traditionally, the role of the middle manager and supervisor has been to control and direct the behavior of others. These managers were supposed to have all the answers and to solve all problems. In this role the manager was the "hero." Implementing RapidResponse management requires a total reorientation of these managers. The manager becomes a combination of coordinator, developer, mentor, and motivator. There is less directing and more leading.

Despite talk about participative management, managers feel that their value and identity are tied to the *control* they exercise over subordinates. And despite a lot of rhetoric about teamwork, managers are oriented toward the idea of the *individual as hero*; individualism, rather than teamwork, is the prevailing management paradigm. The fact that coercive management worked in the past leads managers to believe that coercive methods are still effective.

In the old management paradigm the manager could be indifferent to what subordinates felt, as long as they performed adequately. In the RapidResponse enterprise, on the other hand, the relationships to be managed are more dynamic and intricate than the relationships in the traditional bureaucratic organization. The manager needs a felt sense of the group and its needs, and subordinates need to have a direct role in improving work processes.

"Too Old to Learn Basketball"

When George Williams became CEO of a manufacturing company that was steeped in over 80 years of tradition, he knew that he was taking on a tough challenge. He decided to introduce participatory management practices. These new practices, including methods for documenting quality, had been dictated by the customer to which the manufacturing company sold parts. George quickly realized that his managers had what he referred to as "happy ears"—they would listen to what George had to say, tell him what he wanted to hear, and then go out and do what they had always done. These were hardworking managers who knew, at an intellectual level, that they needed to change their ways. However, they had been conditioned in the "direct and control" way of managing for many years. They were stuck in the old management paradigm. One of these managers, a 30-year veteran, used a sports analogy to explain his dilemma: "For many years I learned to do what was expected, to play the game of baseball. Now I find out after all these years that the game has changed, that we are now expected to play basketball. I think I'm too old to learn basketball." This sports analogy captures the challenge confronting middle-level managers in older established companies.

INFLUENCE OF THE MILITARY MODEL
ON MANAGEMENT

The language of management reflects how deeply the military model has influenced business organizations. Managers have become prisoners of an outdated vocabulary that describes the people who work with them as subordinates and of an environment in which jobs are defined to be specific, detailed, narrow, and task related. Managers have a "span of control" and are part of a "chain of command." Relationships are thought of as contractual and adversarial. The control concepts described by this language are part of the managerial comfort zone. It is not easy for managers, socialized on the language of command and control, to develop a vocabulary that includes words like colleagues, colearners, and partners. The shift to RapidResponse management requires a new mind-set, new behaviors, and a new skill set.

REEDUCATING THE MIDDLES: A THREE-LEVEL SHIFT

The reorientation of middle managers requires a shift at three levels. While there is no magic technique for getting managers and supervisors who have been schooled in old management techniques to embrace the concepts of the RapidResponse enterprise, the broad outlines of the new role are beginning to take shape. What follows is a brief description of the shift that must take place at each of the three levels.

The Shift in Mind-set

As illustrated in Figure 9.2, RapidResponse management requires a major shift in thinking by middle-level managers.

The new high-performance work environment requires that

- The manager or supervisor have a *business* mentality. The manager welcomes opportunities for entrepreneurial activity.
- The manager see employees as an asset that needs to be developed to full potential. The manager has a belief and trust in employees.

The Old Mind-set	*RapidResponse* Mind-set
I am the boss.	I am a *coach*.
People are a liability.	People are an *asset*.
I must have the answers.	*We* need to find answers.
You do as I say.	How can I *help* you?

Figure 9.2
Changes in mind-set required of middle managers.

- The manager thinks of himself or herself as a mentor who encourages creativity and risk taking among employees. Inspiring others to search for answers is seen as a key responsibility.
- The manager see himself or herself as a resource person who is willing to cross departmental or functional boundaries to support people in the group.

THE SHIFT IN *BEHAVIORS*

As illustrated in Figure 9.3, the transition to RapidResponse management requires fundamental changes in *behavior* on the part of middle managers.

The new high-performance work environment requires that managers

- Be willing to provide members of the work group with relevant information and support.
- Be able to let go of "control." This requires developing a high degree of tolerance for uncertainty.
- Have the ability to bring out the best in people. This requires the ability to *manage by expectations.*
- Are able to effectively move across departmental and functional barriers in making things happen.

Old Style Behavior	*RapidResponse* Style
Acts as "lone ranger."	Acts as a team player.
Tightly controls information.	Shares information
Demands conformity.	Encourages diversity.
Maintains the status quo.	Encourages innovation.

Figure 9.3.
Changes in behavior required of middle managers.

Traditional Skills	New Skills
Ability to set goals.	Ability to develop share vision.
Ability to speak well.	Ability to listen.
Ability to develop self.	Ability to develop the group.
Ability to solve problems.	Ability to facilitate team problem solving.

Figure 9.4.
Changes in skill requirements for middle managers.

The Shift in *Skills*

Figure 9.4 illustrates the new *skills* that will need to be acquired as RapidResponse management practices are introduced.

Skills that are especially needed in the high-performance work environment include

- The ability to *tune in* to the wants and needs of members of the work group
- The ability to *communicate* a shared vision for the business unit
- An orientation toward continuously broadening skills and developing new expertise
- Adeptness at team facilitation and expertise in problem solving and decision making

LETTING GO IS HARD TO DO

Change does not come easily to managers who have climbed the corporate ladder through sheer personal drive and a hands-on style that borders on benevolent dictatorship. It is difficult psychologically and philosophically for those managers to recognize that their role has shifted from being a director and order-giver to becoming more an educator and motivator. One of the toughest things for old-style managers to learn is that empowerment of subordinates does not mean abdication of responsibility. It's just the execution that is different, with communication and consensus building becoming paramount. Lower-level employees have more freedom, but they also have more responsibility.

Managers who yield control to empowered subordinates usually become the strongest advocates of the new approach. These managers learn how to take less pride in their own accomplishments and more in the members of the team.

The new attitude is not something that can be forced on managers. Each manager must be given support as he or she moves through a difficult psychological process. Typically the manager moves through three stages:

1. *Fear and resistance.* This is the normal response from people when they are asked to try out new and unfamiliar behaviors.
2. *Reluctant acceptance.* The fear gives way to a tentative acceptance of the new approach. Positive reinforcement is essential at this stage.
3. *Advocacy of employee empowerment.* Managers discover that the new approach allows them to be much more effective in accomplishing company goals.

Each manager will move through the three-stage process at his or her own pace. In our work we have found that age and educational level have little effect on the openness of the individual manager to the new approach. In older companies, it is not unusual to find "old-timers" leading the move to the more participative forms of management.

GET THE MIDDLES SIGNED ON

One of the lessons of the failed quality improvement programs, from quality circles to total quality management, is that the middles must be on board if a program is to succeed. The three revolutionary concepts of RapidResponse management cannot be successfully introduced into a traditionally managed company without the support of department heads, functional managers and supervisors. This middle layer of management can be compared to the civil service. They are the ones that know how to make things happen. They are a reservoir of experience and knowledge. They must be directly involved in any efforts to build a high-performance enterprise. These managers must be given support in reorienting themselves toward a new role in the organization.

Executives leading the transformation effort are faced with a difficult challenge. They know that changing the attitudes, beliefs, and behaviors of people, including middle managers, is a difficult and complex task. They also know that in certain instances they don't have the luxury of spending several years bringing about a change in the way the company is operated. In response to this challenge Deevy Gilligan International developed a "blitz method" for accelerating the process of cultural transformation.

The blitz change strategy, described in the next chapter, outlines a five-step process for bringing about a total transformation of company culture within a six- to nine-month time frame. One of the indispensable steps in this process involves getting the "middles" to abandon "direct-and-control" management in favor of a role that more resembles that of the coach in professional sports. As the "culture carriers," the middles must be supported in making changes if they are to buy in to the new management practices. Any strategy that ignores middle management will be doomed to failure.

Creating the Resilient Organization:
Lesson 9

In the resilient organization, the energy of managers is focused on responding to the marketplace, not on monitoring the activities of others. Managers who were indoctrinated with old-style bureaucratic management principles need to develop a new mind-set and a new set of management skills. If they are to embrace RapidResponse Management principles they will need to undergo a process of reeducation.

CHAPTER 10

CHANGING THE *WHOLE* ORGANIZATION:
A "Blitz" Strategy

There is an exercise frequently used in team building that makes clear the relationship between planning and implementing a task. The goal is to build a construction using Tinkertoys. In a variation of this exercise one group is asked to do the planning and construction as a team, while in the other group the task is divided into two activities—one carried out by the "planners" and the other carried out by the "implementers." The results of this exercise are predictable: *When everyone works together on planning and implementation the project is completed much faster.* Another lesson can be learned from this exercise: When people are involved in planning an activity, they become more committed to the implementation.

The blitz change strategy, pioneered by Deevy Gilligan International (DGI) over an eight-year study period, gets the entire organization involved in planning the future of the enterprise. The process of change is greatly accelerated because everyone is involved in the design phase. Because all employees are involved, they are much more willing to accept the changes.

Over a period of time, the DGI consulting group has made adjustments on their strategy for implementing RapidResponse concepts. Initially, our efforts at implementing the new practices were targeted toward management. After helping top managers come to a consensus, we would typically conduct a series of one- to two-day team-building workshops for middle managers and supervisors. This process of bringing about a change in company culture could take two to three years. Increasingly, clients were asking if the change process could be accelerated. In many instances, management did not feel that they had the luxury of engaging in a process that could take up to three years. It was out of these requests from client organizations that we set about designing an accelerated change strategy. We quickly realized that an effective strategy would require "blitzing" the *entire organization* with the new concepts.

The blitz change strategy, as presented here, can be implemented within a six- to nine-month time frame and is designed to involve everyone in creating the RapidResponse enterprise. This model involves an intensive organizationwide intervention that constitutes a form of shock therapy. Unlike traditional incremental change strategies implemented over several years, the paradigm shift occurs during a 2–3-day meeting of stakeholders.

One of my relatives who worked as a nurse in a city in England during World War II, frequently speaks of the experience of being blitzed by the German bombers. She has described to me how that shared experience brought people together who had previously been strangers. Out of the suffering emerged a sense of unity and purpose among citizens of different religions and socioeconomic backgrounds. In the mind of my relative the word "blitz" has come to mean a unique experience in solidarity. The word has a similar meaning when we use it here to describe a strategy for creating a new consciousness within a work organization.

THE BLITZ CHANGE STRATEGY: A FIVE-STAGE PROCESS

The blitz model, developed by Deevy Gilligan International, offers a systematic approach to introducing RapidResponse principles into a traditionally managed business. It is implemented in five sequential stages, with each stage designed to advance the business on the road toward becoming a RapidResponse enterprise.

Future Search Technology

For many years I believed with others in my profession that no really significant change could be brought about in the culture of an organization without a three- to five-year effort. This was conventional wisdom among Organizational Development (OD) professionals. However, it became increasingly obvious that companies often did not have three-plus years to make essential changes. Recent efforts to bring about an acceleration of the change process have been referred to as "future search" technology. The model developed by DGI is derivative of these efforts. One of the pioneers in the "future search" field is Marvin Weisbord. His book, *Discovering Common Ground: Strategic Futures Conferences for Improving Whole Systems* (San Francisco: Berrett-Koehler, 1993), has become the "bible" of future search practitioners. A more recent publication, *Real Time Strategic Change* (San Francisco: Berrett-Koehler, 1994), by Robert Jacobs has valuable information for anyone considering using this technology. Pioneering work has also been undertaken by Dick Axelrod and his associates, developers of the conference model (The Axelrod Group, Wilmette, Illinois 60091). A less structured approach has been developed by Harrison Owen, originator of *Open Space* Technology.

While future search technology offers the possibility of bringing about a quick transformation in the way a business is managed, its use demands special skills and experience. A solid background in the behavioral sciences and an understanding of the dynamics of change are clear requirements on the part of any consultant or manager who would use this technology.

Each of the five stages in implementing the blitz model, as illustrated in Figure 10.1, will be described in the following sections. The model can be customized to meet the particular needs of the organization.

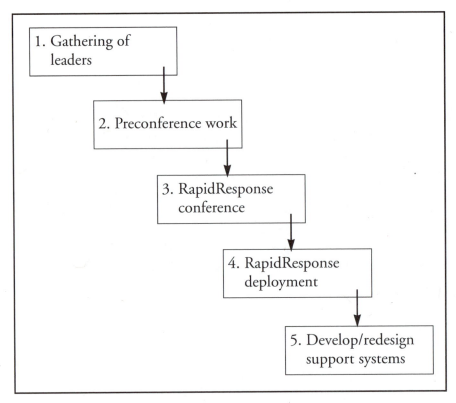

Figure 10.1.
The five-stage blitz model.

STAGE 1. GATHERING OF LEADERS

A brief description of the *Gathering of Leaders Workshop* was provided in Chapter Seven. The leaders of the business come together at an off-site location for a two- to three-day visioning workshop. Focusing on positioning the organization to be successful in a highly dynamic marketplace, the leaders review the internal capabilities of the business and the resources available with a view to identifying changes that need to be made. Leaders return from the visioning session with a clear sense of direction and a commitment to implementing RapidResponse management practices.

In some cases it is appropriate to have a *culture analysis* conducted prior to the *Gathering of Leaders*.

The Culture Analysis

The most effective way to find out what people are thinking and feeling throughout the organization is to conduct a *culture analysis*. The culture analysis provides a snapshot of the climate that exists at any given time. Questions addressed include the following:

Is there cooperation among employees?

Do employees feel recognized and rewarded?

Do employees feel they have a say in how the work gets done?

Do employees feel free of unnecessary policies and procedures?

Do employees feel challenged by the work that they do?

In our work with client organizations we combine a written survey with focus group discussions and one-on-one interviews with selected "culture carriers." Each one-hour focus group includes five to ten employees from the same level within the organization. Participants are given assurances of confidentiality and promised feedback after the data are analyzed. The completed culture analysis provides a clear picture of what people at various levels are feeling and thinking at a given time. More important, the culture analysis pinpoints the culture barriers that will have to be overcome in introducing RapidResponse management practices.

STAGE 2. PRECONFERENCE WORK

Before bringing the whole organization into the room for the RapidResponse conference, it is usually necessary to do preliminary work. Typically, the preconference work includes the following:

1. *Middle management orientation.* As I have indicated in Chapter Nine, the most likely source of resistance to the "new thinking" will come from the middle managers and supervisors. An

overnight retreat, where fears and concerns can be expressed, always pays a rich dividend in the end. The off-site session provides an opportunity to reenforce the team orientation that is an integral part of RapidResponse management.

2. *Customer/supplier focus group.* This one- to two-day miniconference brings together a team made up of representatives of key departments and a representative group of customers and suppliers. A methodology developed by Japanese manufacturing companies, known as quality function deployment (QFD), provides an ideal framework for clearly identifying the wants and needs of customers/suppliers. The DGI consulting group have adapted this methodology for use in service organizations. One feature of the customer/supplier focus group is that it always provides surprises; despite perhaps long involvement with particular customers, managers, and employees are rarely able correctly to predict and prioritize their wishes and needs.

While the customer/supplier focus group is mentioned here as occurring immediately before the RapidResponse conference, it is sometimes advisable to schedule this event at the very beginning of the process—before the *Gathering of Leaders*. What is of paramount importance is that qualitative data on customer wants and needs be available when employees meet in the RapidResponse conference. We sometimes recommend that customers be invited to directly contribute to the RapidResponse conference itself.

3. *Competitive benchmarking.* This is a process of comparing the company's operations against those of other firms. Typically, the comparison is made with those firms believed to exhibit the most efficient operations. Benchmarking speed to market is particularly useful. The need for a formal benchmarking process will depend on how much competitive data are already available.

The Customer Focus Group

While the customer focus group can be customized to meet the unique needs of each organization, there are a few general guidelines to keep in mind. This list is based on real-life experiences.

1. Use an outside facilitator—someone perceived as neutral.

2. Plan the whole scenario, down to the smallest detail.

3. Reduce defensiveness by going through a "practice session." Customers are not likely to give honest feedback if their input is greeted with a defensive response.

4. Avoid "solutionism" during the session: The purpose is data gathering.

5. Make sure that there are no interruptions. Ideally, the session should be held at an off-site location.

6. Remember—you want to identify real *wants* and *needs*. Be prepared for surprises.

STAGE 3. THE RAPIDRESPONSE CONFERENCE

After the leaders have clarified the vision for the future and the other preliminary work has been completed, the organization is ready for the RapidResponse conference. The conference is a meeting of the organization's stakeholders. Included in the conference are members from all levels and departments. Participants explore common ground, develop a shared understanding of the direction for the future, and identify ways of increasing the responsiveness of the organization to the marketplace.

Ordinarily, the conference lasts two days. In organizations that are already oriented toward RapidResponse management, it should be possible to accomplish the goals in a one-day session. Each conference can accommodate 75 to 150 participants; larger organizations will require several conferences to accommodate all employees willing to participate. Participation should be voluntary, except for management. The goal is to get a critical mass committed to the new direction. Those who do not participate are given a complete briefing on what transpired at the conferences.

The conference begins with participants developing an understanding of the organization's history and current situation. Data provided to them come from three sources:

1. *The culture audit.* Information is presented in summary form, with the focus on factors that could have an impact on performance or productivity.

2. *The Customer/supplier focus group.* The prioritized list of needs and wants of customers is presented in such a way as to identify major opportunities for process improvement. Customers may also speak directly to conference participants. If competitive benchmarking has been undertaken, this information should also be presented.

3. *The Gathering of Leaders.* The leadership of the business communicate their vision of the direction for the future. Strategic planning information should also be presented at the conference.

The data supplied to conference participants provide a basis for the exploration of ways to improve the flow of activity within the organization. By the end of the conference, each participant:

- Has a clear understanding of the direction for the future
- Has a solid understanding of "the business of the business"
- Has a strong commitment to helping the company achieve its goals
- Can identify key business processes and understand how to streamline the flow of activity

The role of the steering committee.

The steering committee is made up of representatives of major stakeholder groups, including unions, within the organization. This committee plays a major role in planning and conducting the RapidResponse conference. They collect and synthesize the data generated at the conferences and arrange for the detailed briefing of employees who do not attend.

The expertise and perspective of external consultants is an asset in the planning and implementation of the RapidResponse conference. However, there must also be a high level of involvement by people from within the company. The goal is to have a close, collaborative partnership between the external consultants and the members of the steering committee.

RapidResponse conference—four basic requirements.

Planning and executing a RapidResponse conference is not something that can be reduced to a list of do's and don'ts. It is a highly dynamic event that needs to be skillfully managed. There are, however, several basic requirements that apply to almost every situation. Planning and conducting a RapidResponse conference is a major undertaking. However, it has the potential to generate extraordinary enthusiasm and commitment. The conference can become the defining moment as the organization seeks to move from the old way of doing things to the new RapidResponse mode. Here are four guidelines to keep in mind:

1. *Do detailed preconference planning.* Every detail of the two-day event should be planned. To the casual observer, the conference may seem like a spontaneous unstructured experience; in my experience, however, the most creative and energizing learning experiences are usually the direct result of a scenario that had been very carefully thought through prior to the conference. Preplanning includes everything—the number and "mix" of people in break-out groups, guidelines for discussions, and the amount of time for reporting back to the whole "community."

Wherever possible written instructions are provided to facilitate the process.

2. *Build and maintain momentum.* The conference must impact on people at an emotional as well as an intellectual level. While it does not have to resemble a religious revival meeting, it should generate excitement and enthusiasm. A well-planned conference builds toward creating an environment where the creative juices flow. A fast-paced conference helps maintain the momentum; generally, no activity should be scheduled to last more than one hour, and reports from break-out groups should be limited to not more than 2 minutes. Presentations to the group should generally not exceed 15 minutes and should be delivered using effective audiovisual techniques. These presentations should be well rehearsed before the conference.

3. *Trust the process.* This is a concept that people with limited experience in organizational dynamics find difficult to embrace. In the RapidResponse conference there is no need for hand-holding. Give clear directions and participants will act responsibly. Break-out groups that are limited to seven participants function very well without expert facilitation.

4. *Make the conference an enjoyable experience.* The best team building comes from playful activities that have a physical dimension. Skits are a powerful vehicle for expressing feelings. Use a variety of media, including music.

STAGE 4. RAPIDRESPONSE DEPLOYMENT

RapidResponse conferences generate openness and enthusiasm throughout the organization. It is important that arrangements be made to provide a detailed briefing for employees who did not attend one of the conferences. The major challenge at this stage is to institutionalize the three core RapidResponse concepts and to maintain the momentum generated at the conferences.

An effective mechanism for maintaining organizationwide enthusiasm and commitment is through the use of task forces.

Leadership in deploying and institutionalizing RapidResponse concepts is provided by three task forces, each representative of all major constituencies within the organization. The task forces take up where the conferences end. Their responsibility is to insure that the talk is translated into action. An effective follow-up to the conferences will include a concentrated effort in the following three areas:

1. *Task force on business literacy.* This task force, composed of representatives of all major employee groups, has the responsibility for developing systems and procedures for ensuring that all employees have access to information on "the business of the business." They analyze current communication channels and develop recommendations.

2. *Task force on business process redesign.* This task force, representing all employee groups, has the responsibility for identifying Key Business Processes that need streamlining. They establish and provide support for teams involved in the redesign of key processes. This task force can evolve into a steering committee with ongoing responsibility for creating free-flowing work processes throughout the organization.

3. *Task force on compensation.* Like the other task forces, this group is also representative of the entire organization. If the company has labor unions they should be represented. The task force should include expertise on compensation systems. If this expertise is not available in-house, the company should consider using the services of an outside consultant. The task of this group is to develop innovative ways of helping employees become invested in the company. The task force will lead the way in developing ways of helping employees feel a sense of ownership and responsibility for the success of the company. They will pioneer new ways of "giving each employee a stake in the outcome."

The key challenge during stage 4 is the maintenance of continuous communication with all employees. This can be done through a variety of media—special reports from the CEO, a regular newsletter, E-mail, bulletin boards, and "town meetings." In the blitz change model the goal is to maintain a high level of organizationwide activity during the months after the conferences. Effective communication is the key to maintaining employee interest and commitment.

Task Force Guidelines

We have found that an *organizationwide* task force is one of the most effective tools that can be used to sustain involvement and momentum after conducting a RapidResponse conference. There are a few simple guidelines to keep in mind in establishing a task force. A short list would include the following:

1. Include representation from all major constituencies, including top management.
2. The mandate for the task force should be stated in a clear written statement. This statement should originate with the chief executive officer or president.
3. The time frame for accomplishing the task needs to be clearly specified.
4. Resources needed to accomplish the task must be provided. This will include time to hold meetings. Some groups will need the services of a trained facilitator.

STAGE 5. CREATE SUPPORT SYSTEMS

All the activities in stages 1–4 can be completed within a six-month time frame. Since the strategy is to blitz the entire organization with the new ideas, management must be prepared to give the effort their undivided attention. The challenge is to maintain a high level of productivity while at the same time managing the change process. When a culture change process that ordinarily requires three to four years is thus condensed into six months, it is essential that systems be put in place that will support the new culture. If the gains are not solidified there is a danger of reverting to old attitudes and assumptions. A sec-

---

Five-Stage Blitz Model

1. Gathering of Leaders

The Task: 1. Gain top management commitment to change effort.
2. Identify needed cultural changes.
3. Develop a vision of how the future organization will look.

2. Preconference Work

The Task: 1. Gain commitment of middle management to change effort.
2. Collect data on customers and competitors.

3. RapidResponse Conferences

The Task: 1. Gain organizationwide commitment to new concepts.
2. Get organization unstuck and moving forward.

4. RapidResponse Deployment

The Task: 1. Deployed and institutionalized RapidResponse concepts.
2. Maintain organizationwide employee involvement.

5. Creating Support Systems

The Task: 1. Put the RapidResponse infrastructure in place.
2. Create the learning organization.

Figure 10.2.
The blitz model for organizational change.

ond *Gathering of Leaders*, at the end of the six-month implementation period, can be useful in ensuring that an infrastructure to support the new ways of doing business is in place.

The process of building the RapidResponse enterprise does not end with the implementation of the five-stage blitz change strategy. There will be need for constant innovation in an environment that is continuously changing. The organization will need to evolve into what is known as a *learning organization*. The steps involved in institutionalizing learning will be described in Chapter Fourteen.

DO NOT USE THE BLITZ STRATEGY AS A "QUICK FIX"

As I have stated in earlier chapters, "quick fixes" can create the illusion of change. However, the new marketplace, with its "be quick or be dead" imperative, has created the need for a strategy that can *quickly and effectively* bring about culture change. The blitz change strategy, pioneered by Deevy Gilligan International, speaks to this need for timely results; however, it should not be considered an "easy" fix. What makes this approach attractive to management is that it combines decreased time in implementation with increased commitment by all stakeholders. Of course, without adequate preparation and well-planned follow-up, the blitz strategy could become just another "quick fix."

Creating the Resilient Organization: Lesson 10

Traditional work organizations can be transformed quickly through an exiting new methodology known as the *future search conference*. Because this approach represents a form of "shock treatment" we refer to it as the *blitz strategy*. It is a dynamic five-stage process that has a sudden and powerful impact on the *whole* organization.

C H A P T E R   1 1

UNDERSTANDING RESISTANCE TO CHANGE:
The "Roots" Perspective

The television miniseries "Roots" caused widespread soul searching about the impact of ancestry on attitudes and behaviors. Haley's reconstruction of family history is a powerful reminder of the importance of looking at human behavior from the historical perspective. Sometimes it is necessary to go back several generations, as Haley did, to understand why things are the way they are. I believe that an understanding of how work organizations came to be the way they are is a prerequisite for bringing about major changes. In this chapter I'll show how the traditional bureaucratic work organization, invented in the nineteenth century, is having a devastating impact on worker morale and performance at the end of the twentieth century.

Managers are often baffled by the intensity of resistance to change. They fail to understand the degree to which work organizations are prisoners of their past. More important, these managers fail to understand that the lack of ownership and commitment on the part of workers can be traced to deeply held assumptions that go back 200 years. When we talk of "reinventing organizations" we are talking of undoing practices that have evolved since the industrial revolution.

The "roots" perspective is essential in trying to understand the behavior of social groups, including work organizations. It is interesting to ask, for example, why most business organizations are shaped like a pyramid. Why do people at the top make decisions? Why do people at the bottom sometimes distrust the people at the top? To find the answers to these questions, it is necessary to search for the "roots" of the work organization as we know it today.

My interest in the impact of the past on the present has its origins in work as a change consultant to established companies in the United States and Europe. These consulting experiences led me to reflect on how work organizations had evolved and the degree to which a tradition of "direct and control" management impacted modern business enterprises. I began to understand the extent to which nineteenth-century assumptions were still having a powerful influence on the way people behaved in work organizations at the end of the twentieth century. The investigation into the influence of the past represented a personal search for answers.

First impressions of American enterprise, as a young person, were those of an outsider looking in. Back in Ireland in the 1950s, I had heard my father's stories of working in New York during the Great Depression. The stories had a decidedly pro-union bias, and I came to believe that management and employees were adversaries in America. Paradoxically, my father greatly admired American entrepreneurship. Thus, my father, like many Irish, looked toward the United States with a mixture of envy and respect: The word "America" was synonymous with economic power; products with the "Made in the USA" label were considered prize possessions.

Initial impressions were confirmed after coming to the United States in the early 1960s. Here was a dynamic economy of extraordinary vitality. It seemed that the Americans could do anything; there was no goal that could not be accomplished. When President Kennedy proposed sending a man to the moon, the response was "Why not?" a natural expression of the optimism, national pride, and invincibility of the Americans.

In the 1960s Americans still continued to take economic preeminence for granted, and I, like others, did not pay much attention to how the United States had reached this position. It was not until

20 years later that I seriously began to explore the story of how business organizations had evolved and what factors had contributed to their decline. My search for the "roots" of American business success began with a visit to Heritage Park in Lowell, Massachusetts. What I learned in Lowell and in the other industrial cities of New England, and at the museum of American History in Washington, sheds light on the management of modern work organizations: *The key to understanding modern management could be found in the beginnings of the industrial revolution.*

It was in the industrial cities of the Northeast United States that work organizations as we now know them first took shape. In Lowell's factories and woolen mills, technology and workers were united into enterprises of mass production. These enterprises had two classes of people: the people who did the physical work and the foremen and managers who did the intellectual work, offering direction and control. The system was hierarchical and the management style was dictatorial. Because working conditions were oppressive, relations between the worker and management were adversarial.

The Exploitation of Young Women

One of the most unusual of the national parks is located within the City of Lowell, just 20 miles west of Boston. Known as Heritage Park, it was developed by the U.S. government to preserve the memory of industrial life in the early eighteenth century. A visit to one of the restored mills is a sobering experience. It was here that young farm girls worked ten hours a day, six days a week, in deafening surroundings. Weekly compensation was $1 and free board in dormitories that severely restricted personal freedom. Preserved in the Heritage Park museum are documents that describe the oppressive working conditions of these young women. This national park provides the visitor with valuable insights into the "roots" of the modern work organization. Anyone who wants to understand why the "us" and "them" culture is so deeply embedded in work organizations should visit Heritage Park in Lowell, Massachusetts.

During the industrial revolution, the bureaucratic organization first took shape. And the enterprises of mass production, with their command style of management and hierarchical structure, are direct ancestors of the modern business organization.

BREAD AND ROSES

Fifteen miles north of Lowell is another old industrial city called Lawrence. Each Labor Day weekend the people of Lawrence commemorate a strike by mill workers in 1911, celebrated as an heroic struggle by an earlier generation of workers to overcome oppressive conditions. The celebration is called the Bread and Roses Festival, in tribute to the women who brought bread and roses to their husbands and brothers during that bitter struggle.

This annual Labor Day celebration in Lawrence is a reminder of the time when the relationship between workers and owners was one of distrust and fear. However, modern work organizations, though "kinder and gentler" versions of the original bureaucratic organization, still encourage a gap between those who do the managing and those who do the work. The "us" and "them" culture in the work organizations of today can be traced back to the adversarial relationship that typified the mills and factories.

Heritage Park in Lowell and the Bread and Roses Festival in Lawrence are cited here because they give a "feel" for what work organizations were like for earlier generations of workers. A closer look at how the bureaucratic organization evolved will provide a deeper understanding of present-day work organizations.

BIRTH OF THE BUREAUCRATIC ORGANIZATION

The term bureaucratic organization, as it is used here, refers to the traditional top-down work organization that has its roots in the industrial revolution, and that has been the predominant model for almost 200 years. It is the basic model that can still be found in manufacturing plants, hospitals, insurance companies, and other places of work.

In the early nineteenth century, as industrialization progressed, artisans were replaced by factory workers. This presented the owners of the original industrial plants with a host of technological and human relations problems that were previously unimaginable. Because no formal management system yet existed, owners developed systems based on guesswork and hunches. In fact, the top-down command style of management adapted by work organizations resembled the military model: The people at the top exercised control over those below them; the people at the bottom learned to keep their mouths shut and follow instructions; the people in the middle found themselves pulled in different directions. Despite the tradition for freedom and democracy in American society, life in the factories and mills was characterized by coercion, intimidation, and rigid adherence to company policies.

The man most responsible for shaping the industrial work organization as we know it was an American named Frederick Winslow Taylor. In 1911, Taylor published a monumental work entitled *Shop Management*. In a very short time, Taylor emerged from complete obscurity as a steel works machinist to worldwide prominence as an industrial engineer. His acclaimed theory, which he called "scientific management," asserted that "every single act of every workman can be reduced to a science." Taylor claimed that through scientific measurements, the single "best" method of performing any given job could be identified.

Taylor's work had immediate impact. Jobs were designed in such a way as to require the least amount of skill and intelligence. It was assumed that, since workers did not have education, they lacked intelligence. One of Taylor's associates stated that "it is the aim of scientific management to reduce men *to act as nearly like machines as possible.*" Jobs were designed that required mechanistic and highly repetitive behavior and people became mere extensions of the machine. Owners and managers even began to speculate about a time when they might be able to completely dispense with the use of workers!

Scientific Management

Hardly a competent workman can be found who does not devote a considerable amount of time to studying how slowly he can work and still convince his employer that he is going at a good pace. Under our system a worker is told just what he is to do and how he is to do it. Any improvement he makes upon the orders given to him is fatal to his success.

Frederick Taylor, 1911

Taylor's ideas on segmenting work were reinforced by Max Weber's ideas on what a bureaucratic organization should look like. Weber, a German sociologist, identified the characteristics of an ideal bureaucracy. The complex organizational charts that can be found in most larger companies are a testimony to the influence of Weber. The ideas of Taylor and Weber are the conceptual foundation on which the bureaucratic organization was built, and *these old ideas still dominate the workplace.*

THE TRIUMPH OF AMERICAN INDUSTRY

The bureaucratic organization, despite its shortcomings, flourished throughout the first half of the twentieth century. The extraordinary productive capacity of American enterprise was evident during World War II when thousands of planes and ships were manufactured and built, often in a matter of weeks or even days. Within a period of 100 years, America had developed from a farming community to an economic superpower. The supremacy of U.S. industry continued into the 1960s.

The moon landing, more than any other event, signified that America had become the dominant and unchallenged economic power in the world; that historic event was the crowning achievement of American industry.

The moon landing signified that America had become the dominant and unchallenged economic power in the world.

Many have interpreted the great achievements of America's industrial machine as a testimonial to the success of the bureaucratic organization with its command-and-control management. The "record" is impressive: two world wars won and landing a person on a distant planet. However, *greatness was achieved despite the fact that there was very little worker involvement* in decision making or problem solving; it was assumed that profits would go to owners and investors and that workers would be compensated with a fixed basic wage. Implicit in the two-class work environment was the idea that management and workers had mutually exclusive interests. The adversarial relationship between workers and company management, reflected in the power of the unions, was accepted as one of the "givens" of industrial life.

In retrospect, it seems remarkable that extraordinary achievements were accomplished despite a work environment characterized by mutual distrust.

The core assumptions about the rights and responsibilities of workers and management, and the idea that work organizations should be shaped like a pyramid with people at the upper levels directing the activities of people at lower levels, went largely unquestioned from the beginnings of the industrial revolution until the middle of the twentieth century. Because the bureaucratic organization, with its command-and-control management, was instrumental to America's attainment of global supremacy, *there was little incentive to look for alternative models of management.* In the 1960s, competitive pressures were almost nonexistent: Japanese cars were rusting in the showrooms, British cars had defective electrical systems, and German "bugs" were considered unsafe on any highway.

Indeed, the bureaucratic organization, as we have come to know it, became so closely identified with the American way of life that any criticism would have seemed un-American. By the 1970s, scapegoating union leadership had become a popular political activity. President Ronald Reagan's firing of the air traffic controllers in 1981 was widely applauded. The general consensus was that, despite some shortcomings, the bureaucratic organization was not broken and did not need fixing.

THE OTHER SIDE TO THE STORY

Because of its spectacular accomplishments, there has been a reluctance to recognize the downside to the bureaucratic organization. The person who first challenged the basic assumptions on which the bureaucratic organization is built was an M.I.T. professor named Douglas McGregor. In his classic work, *The Human Side of Enterprise*, published in 1960, McGregor suggested that the bureaucratic organization is fatally flawed. He concluded that traditional work organizations, with their control style of management, contain the seeds of their own destruction.

With the dramatic decline in American enterprise over the past 25 years there is now more of a willingness to look at how "command-and-control" management is impacting present-day work organizations. It is obvious that many of these organizations have become dinosaurs—lacking the energy and flexibility to compete in the modern business environment.

With the benefit of hindsight the moon landing in 1969 can be seen as the final chapter in the story of industrialization that began in the cities of New England: The United States was about to enter a period of decline. The period of global preeminence was over. The old paradigm became outdated. The time had come for employees to be "liberated" from an organizational culture that stifled and suffocated.

The first step in the liberation process is an understanding of why the bureaucratic organization, despite its achievements, is destructive of employee initiative, creativity, and productivity. In the following pages I will use the concept of *paradigms* to explain how traditional work organizations sap the energy out of people.

BUREAUCRATIC ORGANIZATIONS
DESTROY INITIATIVE

In a favorite cult movie from the 1960s called *Night of the Living Dead,* scenes showing the "living dead" wandering around aimlessly are a metaphor for what can be found in the workplace: employees whose faces show a lack of interest and who are disengaged. These

Paradigm Paralysis: A Fatal Disease

In his widely distributed videotape, *The Business of Paradigms* (Burnsville, MN: Charthouse Learning, 1990), Joel Barker, a futurist, defines a paradigm as a set of rules that establish boundaries to our thinking on any subject. Barker shows how paradigms, *by filtering information*, make it difficult to see new ideas. This concept has particular applicability in a business environment that is undergoing cataclysmic change.

When the business world undergoes change, only those companies that react quickly will prosper. The ability to react requires an openness to new ideas. To survive, the basic assumptions of business must be reexamined objectively and changed when appropriate. The paradigms of the past must be exposed, reviewed, and changed to those of the future. Organizations blinded by the old rules and unable to see the need for change suffer from what Barker calls *paradigm paralysis*. This is a fatal disease that has destroyed more than a few companies in recent years.

---

employees go through the motions, but their hearts are not in their work. In the "living dead" work environment, employees frequently exhibit the symptoms of stress, including headaches, chemical dependency, and absenteeism. The concept of paradigms is useful in explaining the "living dead" phenomenon.

A *paradigm* is defined as a set of assumptions that forms a pattern or a model of thinking. It is a mental picture we form to define the way we see something. In Chapter One I used the "flat earth paradigm" to explain how paradigms change. Down through the ages, when people thought about the earth they visualized something flat. When Copernicus came along with scientific evidence that contradicted this mental picture, people had trouble letting go of the old mind-set. While paradigms are necessary to our ability to make sense of the world, it is easy to become a prisoner of these paradigms.

The Swiss watchmaking industry has been cited as the classic example of getting blinded by an existing paradigm. For many generations, the Swiss craftsmen thought of the watch as an instrument with mechanical parts. When quartz technology was introduced in the 1960s, the Swiss continued to hold on to the "mechanical watch paradigm." They could not imagine a watch without finely crafted moving parts. The result of this *paradigm blindness* is that the Japanese, by embracing a new paradigm based on quartz technology, were able to become the dominant players in the watchmaking industry.

All of us have had the experience of being blinded by our paradigms when we have formed a mental model that makes it difficult to see beyond the boundaries of the paradigm. *The bureaucratic organization represents a paradigm of management that blinds people from seeing the real potential that individuals can bring to the work environment.*

THE EFFECT OF PARADIGMS ON PERFORMANCE

In his video on paradigms, Joel Barker introduces the concept of the *paradigm effect*. According to Barker the paradigm sets boundaries that powerfully influence human behavior by defining what is possible and what is impossible. As an illustration, Barker mentions the Tarajumarian Indians, who regularly are able to run 60 to 70 miles because the ability to do so fits within the tribal paradigm. He suggests that if any of us were raised in this tribe, we would also easily be able to run that distance. Similarly, the bureaucratic organization, as the widely accepted paradigm of the work environment, has a powerful effect on worker performance by negatively defining possibilities for worker behavior.

Like the Swiss watchmakers, most managers and workers have deep-rooted assumptions about work organizations. These assumptions form a paradigm or mental model that includes such elements as top-down decision making, a multilayered hierarchy, clearly defined functions, and a fixed basic pay. The mental picture is of a pyramid-shaped structure with roles and responsibilities clearly defined.

The bureaucratic organization, as the widely accepted paradigm of the work environment, has a powerful effect on worker performance by negatively defining possibilities for worker behavior.

THE PARADIGM EFFECT:
BILL SMITH GOES TO WORK

The power of the paradigm to impact behavior is illustrated in the case of Bill Smith. An operator at a local manufacturing plant, Smith is a typical employee in that he wants to follow company policies, stay out of trouble, and provide a decent living for his family. Despite his 20-year tenure, he actually knows very little about the company. Like coworkers, he accepts the fact that there is no connection between the amount of energy expended and the compensation received at the end of the week. When it comes to the "business of the business," he is an outsider; most of what Bill knows about the company comes from the rumor mill or the business pages of the newspaper. He sees little connection between what he does each day and the success or failure of the company in the marketplace. Smith finds himself doing work that requires little brain power.

Perhaps the biggest adjustment for Smith in recent years has been the realization that *the promise of job security is no longer valid.* He understands that in the age of mergers, acquisitions, and junk bond–financed buyouts, loyalty and hard work are no guarantee of future employment. He wonders why he should dedicate himself to the success of the company without some opportunity to share in the gains or the assurance of future employment. Clearly, such doubts—well-founded doubts—do not encourage competitive behavior. Boredom and disinterest can be read on the faces of Bill and his coworkers; they seem to be thinking, "Why bother?"

Executives and managers find it difficult to comprehend why a Bill Smith would be bored, disinterested, and lacking enthusiasm for the company. But isn't it self-evident? Bill's lack of motivation is not caused by lack of intelligence, but is directly attributable to the fact that he operates within the boundaries of the *control paradigm.* He does what is expected. He follows directions. The way he behaves is a consequence of the paradigm effect. To change the behavior of Bill Smith and his coworkers requires a new paradigm based on commitment, not on control.

THE PARADIGM EFFECT:
BILL SMITH AT PLAY

To fully appreciate the soul-destroying impact of the *control paradigm,* consider how Bill Smith behaves within a different paradigm, a different set of assumptions about how he should perform. After his day at the factory, Bill goes home, showers, and has supper with his family. Later he joins friends at the local softball field. He finds himself involved in a boisterous but friendly game to decide who will buy the pizza and beer. The competitive juices flow as he and his teammates strive to outperform their opponents. As each hit and each run is accompanied by cheering and backslapping, Bill Smith is transformed from his life among the "'living dead" on the factory floor into a high-energy player committed to giving the maximum effort. When Bill and his teammates get behind a couple of runs, they strive extra hard to get back into the game. *The scorecard has an energizing effect on performance.* His efforts are driven from within, from a desire to be a winner. In the softball park Bill Smith is performing within the boundaries of a very different paradigm—the *commitment paradigm.* He doesn't feel controlled or encumbered; *the drive to perform comes from within.*

The contrast between Bill Smith's performance on the factory floor and his performance on the softball field illustrates the paradigm effect. Because Bill Smith is operating according to a very different set of assumptions on the softball field, his behavior is totally different from his behavior on the factory floor. What if the same assumptions that govern his performance on the softball field were applied to the workplace? The performance of any individual operating within the control paradigm is predictable. Put Bill Smith within an enterprise operated according to the "three secrets" of RapidResponse management, and his performance would be very different. Figure 11.1

The Paradigm Effect

Control Paradigm	Commitment Paradigm
"I hate this job."	"I love this job."
Employee is:	**Employee is:**
Bored	Fulfilled
Working to survive	Playing to win
Responding to external controls	Internally driven
Encumbered by rules	Exercising initiative/creativity
Acting like and outsider	Acting like an owner
Pretending to work	Adding value

Figure 11.1.
How paradigms impact employee performance.

shows how paradigms can greatly impact on the way people feel about the work environment.

THE WORKPLACE PARADIGM MUST CHANGE

For too long the effort has been to change the Bill Smiths rather than recognize that it is the assumptions of the workplace that need to be changed. Workers need to be liberated from an environment that stifles initiative. The old control paradigm, after 200 years, needs to be replaced with a new paradigm that fosters commitment and loyalty. The bureaucratic paradigm, like the flat earth paradigm of the Middle Ages, has outlived its usefulness. A new set of rules is needed for a business environment that requires a quick response to the marketplace, work process flexibility, and a high degree of employee commitment. The core assumptions of RapidResponse management, presented in earlier chapters, provides the foundation for creating a new paradigm based on ownership and commitment.

**Workers need to be liberated from an environment
that stifles initiative.**

THE CHALLENGE:
BECOMING UNSTUCK

This brief review of the impact of past history on present-day work organizations leads to one certain conclusion: Organizations need to undergo a profound change. There is no simple or easy way to bring about a shift in the workplace paradigm. In Chapter Ten I presented a model for helping bring about a total transformation from the old bureaucratic or control paradigm to a new paradigm based on commitment. The question of how to liberate older organizations from a culture that emphasizes dependency will be explored more fully in Chapter Twelve.

Creating the Resilient Organization:
Lesson 11

Our work organizations, as traditionally designed, destroy the enthusiasm and commitment of workers. An understanding of the impact of "command-and-control" management on employee motivation is a requirement for building tomorrow's resilient organization. Employees who are constrained by the requirements of the old bureaucratic management paradigm need to undergo a process of liberation.

C H A P T E R   1 2

THE PSYCHODYNAMICS OF CHANGE:
Letting Go Before Moving Forward

In *Promises to Keep* (New York: Times Books, 1992), Richard Goodwin, a former special assistant to President Kennedy, sets forth a broad agenda for restoring America to its former leadership position as a political and economic superpower. He describes this restoration as the most urgent challenge confronting the American people. Clearly, revitalizing outdated bureaucratic organizations must be part of the larger agenda advocated by Goodwin. However, as suggested in Chapter Eleven, the task of bringing about revitalization is not a simple matter. Since the days when Machiavelli wrote *The Prince*—some 500 years ago—leaders have recognized that major organizational changes would never be popular. People become very invested in current structures. They find themselves entrenched in a comfort zone.

Recently, the challenge to streamline and rebuild has been taken up by a growing number of national leaders including Texas billionaire Ross Perot and Vice President Al Gore. As I have explained, business and industrial institutions can be restored only through *cultural transformation and systems change*. The organization must let go of its past. Incorporating the three core concepts of RapidResponse management in a traditionally managed company requires new thinking about how a company can most effectively be managed.

The key to successful change is to help people take pride in the new system and to make those most affected by the change more comfortable with the new system than they were with the old. This is a formidable task. People fear change. Only by involving employees in the change process can fear be reduced.

For the past decade I have had the opportunity to observe older established companies as they introduced RapidResponse management practices. Invariably—in hospitals, manufacturing plants, financial institutions—management underestimate resistance to change. The dynamics of this *resistance* need to be understood if new ideas are to be successfully introduced into a company.

By directing implementation in client organizations and also by implementing RapidResponse in my own company, I developed common-sense strategies for reducing resistance to change and for getting people to embrace new ideas. These strategies are highly effective in helping any older organization undergo a transformation.

It must be considered that there is nothing more difficult to carry out or more doubtful of success, nor dangerous to handle than to initiate a new order of things.

Machiavelli

Today, companies spend large sums of money on various programs designed to make them more competitive. Consulting companies that sell total quality management and business process reengineering programs are experiencing spectacular growth. And yet, as I have already indicated, over 75% of these programs fizzle out within two years. *They produce dismal results because they fail to bring about a change in the existing culture of the organization.* This chapter will demonstrate why a purely mechanistic approach, that focuses on skills and techniques, is doomed to failure. The *psychological dimensions* of organizational change will be explored. Finally, I will describe concrete strategies that can be used in enabling organizations to move out of the comfort zone and embrace new management practices.

THE PSYCHOLOGY OF RESISTANCE

"We can't let go of our past." This is the way one CEO expressed frustration over the failure of his company to make necessary changes in management practices. Frustration rises when people resolutely resist change even when changes are necessary for survival.

While some business leaders understand that a shift in management practices must be made, they cannot understand why changes that are good for the company encounter intense employee resistance. These leaders fail to appreciate the powerful psychological forces that keep people from letting go of old ideas.

Often, the implementation of change is not successful. I believe the major reason for failure is that the organization and its employees become stuck in what I call the "comfort zone." Few executives truly understand the psychological stress experienced by managers and workers in letting go of the old ways. When people join a work organization, they become socialized into the culture of that organization. They learn that certain behaviors are rewarded. These behaviors become part of the individuals' comfort zone. While it is difficult to get one person to let go of old ways of behaving, changing the ways of an *entire organization* may seem to border on the impossible.

WHY DO CHANGE EFFORTS FAIL?

Executives and managers become frustrated and puzzled when their efforts to introduce change produce dismal results. "Bottom line—nothing has really changed" was the postmortem comment of one executive who had expended considerable energy and financial resources in trying to make her company more market focused. It is useful at this point to enumerate the most common reasons why these efforts fail.

Reason 1. The human dimension of change is not addressed.

Recent attempts to introduce total quality management and business process reengineering provide ample warning of the danger of neglecting the human dimension: Three out of four of these programs "hit the wall" within two years. Because the human side of implementation is neglected, the culture remains the same. Executives are seduced by the promise of quick and painless introduction of new management techniques, everyone stays within their comfort zones, and nothing really changes.

Statistical tools and techniques are not a substitute for genuine cultural change. *The challenge is to transform the organization,* and transforming the organization is primarily a psychological problem of changing attitudes and behaviors.

Reason 2. Deep-rooted dependency behavior is ignored.

One of the most widely held myths is the idea that workers, if given the opportunity, will quickly become more actively involved in the workings of the organization. The reality is that the hierarchically structured enterprise, with its top-down management, has bred *psychological dependency* into people at the lower levels. The evidence of this dependency can be found in almost every business organization. Employees learn that the key to success is to "keep your nose clean" and follow directions. Generations of conditioning have created a workplace in which people are content simply to do what they are told. Psychological dependency becomes a comfort zone that allows employees to opt out on ownership and responsibility and to find psychological sustenance in the norms of the traditional organization. Learning to perform with more independence and autonomy requires rejecting the adversarial relationship between management and workers that has characterized traditional work organizations. It means assuming more responsibility. The patterns of dependency behavior, deeply ingrained in traditional work organizations, are not addressed in TQM and reengineering programs.

Reason 3. Workers continue to distance themselves from company goals.

One of the most valuable insights that I have gained from conducting employee focus groups is the understanding of how workers who have strong loyalty to their own job and work group frequently

Worker Dependence: A Chronic Disease

The phenomenon of *dependence* and its impact on the way people perform in the workplace is rarely understood by managers and consultants. And yet the evidence of chronic employee dependence is everywhere. One of the people who has written most eloquently on this topic is Peter Block. His book, *The Empowered Manager* (San Francisco: Jossey-Bass,1987), should be required for anyone who wants to bring about a transformation of an older organization. Block makes it clear why so many workers choose not to act as adults in the workplace.

have very little loyalty to the company. Employees simply do not identify with the business objectives of the organizations that employ them. The priority placed by employees on individual performance over company goals creates *psychological distance* between the individual and the organization. When the employee is concerned about doing a good job without having an interest in the success of the company, taking pride in his or her work while disassociating from the business, a protective comfort zone is established. Employees who value this psychological distance will have to undergo a major attitudinal adjustment if they are to succeed in an entrepreneurial environment where individual and company success are closely linked. TQM and process reengineering programs invariably ignore the need to create a new psychological bond between the individual worker and the organization.

Reason 4. The fear of new technology is not addressed.

The advent of computer-based technology, with its need for increased intellectual skills, frightens many employees. For them, technology represents a move out of the comfort zone. The idea of doing work with more intellectual content is not attractive to a person who has grown up in a work environment that primarily required physical activity. The new technologies also raise concerns about becoming redundant as work processes are reengineered and jobs are eliminated. Few companies provide help for employees in overcoming their fears of the new technologies.

Reason 5. The infrastructure remains unchanged.

Changing the infrastructure of an established company is a challenge requiring special political skills. This infrastructure includes the written policies contained in the personnel manual and the unwritten rules and norms that govern most organizational behavior. This infrastructure becomes a security blanket by defining roles, responsibilities, and relationships for both workers and managers. In unionized companies, furthermore, workers often consider themselves "protected" from management. Again, many companies introduce various "improvement" programs but fail to make necessary changes in the infrastructure.

Reason 6. The work force remains oriented toward "the good old days."

Some companies that have experienced outstanding success in the past find it difficult to embrace new management practices. It is not unusual to find in these companies a nostalgia for the "good old days" and a hope that somehow the past can be recaptured. This backward focus makes it difficult to move forward. Organizational change programs that fail to reorient the work force toward the future are destined to fail.

WHAT IS NEEDED IS *CULTURE CHANGE*

All the reasons listed earlier for the failure of various change interventions can be reduced to one sentence: *The culture of the organization remains unchanged.* Managers tend to roll their eyes when the concept of culture is introduced into the discussion. They see it as representing the soft side of the organization and as having little impact on competitiveness. These managers prefer to focus on what they consider the "hard stuff."

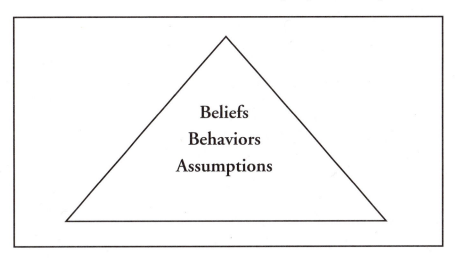

Figure 12.1.
The ingredients of company culture.

As Figure 12.1 illustrates, *culture* is the combination of beliefs, behaviors, and assumptions that make up the psychological infrastructure of the organization. At the heart of culture are the patterns of *shared assumptions* that are learned by members of a group. These assumptions grow out of the efforts of the organization to survive in the external environment while dealing with problems of internal integration. Over time these assumptions become part of what is accepted as "truth" within the organization. In some organizations the core beliefs and assumptions can be traced back to the founders. The behavior of the leader plays a major role in developing the culture of any company.

Any attempt to introduce management practices that are radically different from the existing culture will almost certainly fail if there is incompatibility between the existing culture and the ideas that are introduced. This is why so many of the total quality management efforts fizzled out after a short time. Just as the human body has the tendency to reject new organs, organizations tend to reject new management practices that do not conform to the existing culture. The culture—that sum total of beliefs, behaviors, and assumptions that can be found in any organization—must support the new strategic initiatives if changes are to take hold. *Thus the culture must be changed along with management practices.* Without a shift in the beliefs, behaviors, and assumptions of employees, no new set of skills or work processes will bring about the kind of reform that is needed for today's continuously changing marketplace. The conventional wisdom is that the process of bringing about these changes in an established company takes two to three years. The major reason for developing the blitz change model, as described in Chapter Ten, was to accelerate this process.

CONDITIONS FOR CHANGE TO TAKE PLACE

There are several different ways of describing the process of bringing about a change in culture. It is generally agreed that an organization must be in pain before it can let go of old assumptions and change behavior patterns. Where there is a strong culture, there may need to be extreme pain before change can occur.

Two people who have greatly contributed to our understanding of the psychological processes involved in helping an organization navigate its way through a cultural change are Edgar Schein, an M.I.T. professor, and William Bridges, author of *Transitions: Making Sense of Life's Changes* (Reading, MA: Addison-Wesley, 1980).

Professor Schein identifies three conditions that are required to bring about cultural change:

1. *Disconfirmation.* This is the beginning of the unfreezing process. Management shares information that things are not going well. This might mean telling employees that the company is losing market share or letting them know that a new product has failed.

2. *Induction of guilt/anxiety.* Employees are induced to experience feelings of failure. Management shares how serious things are with employees. Employees are told that management can't turn things around alone.

3. *Creation of psychological safety.* A hopeful vision for the future allows employees to feel safe while going through painful trans-

formation. Employees perceive that there is a way forward, that there is a possible solution or new way to do things.

Schien believes that all three conditions must be met if people are to be motivated to change. If the organization is not experiencing significant pain, changes in culture are unlikely to occur.

William Bridges has conceptualized the process of change for individuals and organizations as moving through three successive stages:

Stage 1. Letting go of the past

Stage 2. The neutral zone

Stage 3. New beginnings

Bridges' key insight is that "letting go" must take place *before* the individual or the organization can move forward. In other words, the people who inhabit the bureaucratic organization must first let go of the old attitudes and behaviors before new RapidResponse concepts can be embraced. If people are stuck in a comfort zone, they must first deal with the issue of getting unstuck. Any effort to introduce high-performance concepts without addressing the need for people to let go of the past will almost certainly fail. This lesson in human psychology is lost on the many business leaders who go charging forward while the work force is still focused on the past. Unfortunately, many TQM and process reengineering consultants, with little background in the social and behavioral sciences, have no appreciation of the psychological changes that are required to bring about a cultural transformation.

THE GORBACHEV LESSON

Gorbachev implicitly recognized the validity of Bridges' concepts when he instituted the policy of glasnost or "loosening up" in the old Soviet Union. He provided a large-scale example of "letting go" as a step in the strategy of introducing a new economic policy. The fact that the economy was in serious trouble was a major factor in the Russian people accepting the reforms. Executives need to pay attention to the Gorbachev lesson: Older established companies will need to be "unfrozen" before introducing RapidResponse management.

Figure 12.2 illustrates the degree of cultural transformation that needs to take place in introducing RapidResponse management. Keep in mind that this transformation involves an essentially psychological process. Attitudes and behaviors need to change. Other important considerations to keep in mind are to

- Lead and *support* people through the change process. When it comes to making cultural change people respond more favorably to persuasion than coercion.
- Understand the need for pain and anxiety. The old "no pain, no gain" axiom has particular relevance when it comes to getting people to let go of the past.
- Don't try to ignore the pull of the past.
- Create a hopeful vision to carry people through the transformation.

Organizational Culture		
Bureaucratic Culture		**RapidResponse Culture**
Individual as hero	>	Team orientation
Focus on "control"	>	Focus on "commitment"
Focus inward	>	Market/customer focus
Psychological dependence	>	Acts like owner
Commitment to own work group	>	Commitment to company
Departmental mind-set	>	Business process orientation
Management centered	>	Employee centered

Figure 12.2.
A comparison between cultures.

STRATEGIES FOR GETTING UNSTUCK

The blitz change strategy, presented in Chapter Ten, describes a high-powered five-stage method for transforming the culture of older businesses. This methodology was developed to meet the needs of work organizations where an accelerated change process is essential for survival. As I indicated in the first chapter of this book, I now favor an approach that gets the total organization involved rather than incremental strategies. The entire organization undergoes a major catharsis and is blitzed with the new management concepts. In designing this model, our consulting group incorporated a series of strategies that have been found to be highly effective in helping organizations through the transformation process.

Some business organizations will opt to develop a customized plan for bringing about cultural change. *The strategies used will be dependent on the readiness of the organization for the new concepts.* A complex variety of factors will affect the level of readiness. The stronger the culture the more difficult it is to bring about change. A customized plan will use a combination of the strategies listed in the paragraphs that follow.

The plan that is developed for bringing about cultural transformation should build on the existing platform. Few companies or institutions will be starting at point zero. A company where employees have a high degree of business literacy will have a head start on "allowing each player to keep score." Similarly, it will be easy to create "free flow" in a company that has already been working on process improvement. The *RapidResponse Readiness Checklist*, found at the end of this book, provides a means for measuring how the organization is performing in relation to each of the three core RapidResponse management practices.

Each of the twelve strategies described in this chapter has been proven effective in helping change in older established companies. Several of these strategies can be used simultaneously.

STRATEGY 1. CREATE CATHARSIS

In psychology the word *catharsis* denotes an emotional discharge of feelings. We have found that in older organizations, employees need a discharge of emotions to unload themselves of "baggage" from the past. The catharsis can be a painful emotional experience. Without a catharsis the organization is unable to move forward. It is analogous to the business having a "born-again" experience. The introduction of RapidResponse concepts requires accepting a new set of beliefs and assumptions. In work with many diverse work organizations, both in the United States and in Europe, we have found that some form of catharsis must take place for an organization to move forward.

Kurt Lewin, a sociologist whose work was published in the 1940s, used the term *unfreezing* to describe what needs to happen before an established organization can change. The best way to bring about the unfreezing or catharsis is to create a sense of crisis. Communicating to employees that the company will face dire consequences if changes are not made is an effective way of getting them to let go of the old thinking.

STRATEGY 2. CONFRONT EMPLOYEES WITH EVIDENCE

How do you get people involved in the change process? There is abundant evidence that people are more willing to support change when they believe their own economic security is threatened. However, employees have a tendency to engage in denial, even when there is evidence that the survival of the organization may be at stake. Management needs to confront employees with the evidence of the need for change. Give people the rationale for change, laying it out in clear dramatic terms. *Everyone* needs to be informed as to why management is introducing new ways of doing business. It is not a question of scaring people but of appealing to their self-interest. In unionized work environments it is of paramount importance that the union leaders be given the facts supporting the case for change. When people understand that they are standing on a burning platform they are much more willing to make difficult personal changes.

STRATEGY 3. START TREATING EMPLOYEES AS ENTREPRENEURS

At the heart of the RapidResponse concept is the notion of employees working for themselves, thereby creating an environment in which

Getting Rid of "Baggage"

The reason why so many business organizations can't make it in the modern business environment is obvious: They are carrying too much "baggage" from the past. How can they dump this "baggage"? They need to experience psychological catharsis. The following exercise can be used to bring about the needed emotional discharge.

Members of the group are divided into smaller groups of five to eight employees. Each group is asked to develop a skit describing "how things used to be around here." This exercise always produces extraordinary creativity on the part of managers and line staff. Some skits illustrate traumatic experiences from the past. Others use humor to describe difficult moments in the life of the organization. Each skit, as it is performed, triggers a discharge of emotions on the part of members of the group. They allow group members to relive the past. The more intense the emotional discharge the more effective the exercise. The laughter and tears help free people from the past and allow them to move forward.

It is recommended that this exercise be conducted at an off-site location, free from distractions. The discussion following presentation of skits should be facilitated by an individual with experience in group and organizational dynamics.

they can put passion, energy, excitement, and motivation into their work. This entrepreneurial activity must be reinforced. Employees must be encouraged to take risks and assume responsibility. As indicated in Chapter Six, one of the most effective ways of reinforcing entrepreneurial behavior is through the compensation system.

Managers and supervisors will need to abandon their parenting roles if they are to effectively encourage entrepreneurial endeavor. Control and manipulation discourage people from risk taking and create dependency on the part of workers. The attitude that "it's just a job" is a direct result of the dependent way that employees have been treated in the bureaucratic organization. Promoting initiative and independence on the part of employees will require a new mind-set on the part of management.

It has been said that the best workers are volunteers. You can't order people to be committed to the success of the enterprise. Employees have to be motivated to perform at peak levels. The leader can create an encouraging environment but the commitment has to come from within the individual.

Here it is appropriate to say something about the *psychology* of changing employee behavior. In their best-selling book *The One Minute Manager*, Blanchard and Johnson explain a basic principle of behavioral science: Behavior that is reinforced will be repeated. A mother teaching her young child to say "Daddy" understands this principle as she reinforces each approximation of the word with a hug or a kiss. The concept of behavioral reinforcement has particular relevance when it comes to helping employees overcome dependency behavior and increase ownership and responsibility. The old patterns of behavior are deeply ingrained. People will not change deep-rooted behavioral patterns simply because they are told to change. The continuous reinforcement of desired behavior by management is a requirement for attitudes and behaviors to change in the workplace.

Strategy 4. Keep Focused on the Big Picture

The lesson of the TQM experience in recent years is very clear: If you want to make significant value-adding changes don't get bogged down in details. The obsession with tools and techniques has led many companies to lose sight of why they were instituting the new management practices in the first place. A major reason why most "process improvement" programs fail within two years is this preoccupation with the microissues. Teaching people how to "do TQM" becomes more important than improving the ability of the business to perform in the marketplace.

The successful introduction of RapidResponse management practices that are described in this book requires a laserlike focus on one goal: the development of an organization that has the *responsiveness* and *agility* to outperform competitors. It makes no sense to burden employees with activities that are not relevant to the accomplishment of this goal. Don't get bogged down in the details! The focus must be on making the essential changes needed to increase competitiveness.

As I have repeatedly stated, the major focus in tomorrow's business environment must be the development of flexibility and agility. While bureaucracy and complexity are enemies to speed and responsiveness, RapidResponse management practices make it possible to adapt and respond quickly. The effort to bring about the transformation from the old bureaucratic way to the new RapidResponse mode must be characterized by an obsession for simplicity and bottom-line results.

Working Hard, Going Nowhere

There are many examples of companies investing heavily in improvement efforts only to gain minimal results. The experience of one large utility company is not unique. A prestigious consulting firm was hired to assist in the introduction of total quality management. Over 70 employees were trained as team facilitators, and numerous workshops were conducted for managers and employees. A well-staffed office was established to support the effort. Hundreds of employees were recruited to serve on process improvement teams.

Two years after the initial introduction of TQM, it was clear to company management that they were getting very little return on their investment. The analysis conducted by Deevy Gilligan International clearly indicated a failure to have any significant impact on organizational performance. It was a case of expending energy and resources on "doing things right" rather than on "doing the right things." Somehow, the effort had become focused on the improvement techniques themselves rather than on the big picture. TQM had become an end in itself.

Strategy 5. Start Sharing Business Information

The importance of sharing business information with rank-and-file employees was explored in Chapter Four. A few comments on operationalizing this concept are appropriate.

The chief financial officer is a key player in initiating a program of business literacy for employees. The first step is teaching all employees how to understand profit and loss statements. Monthly "town meetings" can be an effective vehicle for communicating business information. My experience is that once employees start receiving financial information, they look forward to the regular briefings. They also quickly develop the ability to make sense out of the numbers.

Strategy 6. Make the Customer the Focal Point of Process Activity

Most companies have ordering processes that are too cumbersome, going through too may hands and too many functions—meaning no single person has responsibility for getting services and products to customers. In addition, in most organizations, it's not the customer who is the focal point of employees, it's the boss. The steps used in redesigning a process with the customer as the focal point are described in Chapter Six.

> *There is a nearly unanimous opinion forming that in the 1990's we'll be running businesses primarily by customer-oriented processes.*
>
> Lawrence Bossidy, CEO, Allied Signal

Strategy 7. Start Reinventing the Infrastructure

Each business organization is held together by an infrastructure of policies and procedures. With the introduction of RapidResponse concepts, the policies and procedures need to be rewritten. As a consequence, the senior human resources professional has a key role to play during the period of transition from bureaucratic management to

RapidResponse management. Senior executives must not overlook the importance of the HR manager in the change process, but rather encourage the creation of a new infrastructure that reflects a collaborative relationship between management and worker. The policies and procedures should communicate management's trust and confidence in workers.

STRATEGY 8. FOLLOW THE PATH OF LEAST RESISTANCE

The basic idea here is that side-stepping resistance can sometimes be more effective than confronting it head on. When RapidResponse concepts are introduced strong resistance will be encountered. We have found that this resistance typically comes from one-third of the employees. A strategy that focuses on deemphasizing resistance and mobilizing the efforts of that two-thirds of the people who support change can sometimes be most effective. The forces in support of change need to be stronger than the resistance forces if the organization is to move beyond the status quo.

Force-field analysis is a technique for diagnosing situations that was developed in the 1940s by Kurt Lewin. Figure 12.3 illustrates the competing forces that are present in every change situation. Before embarking on any change strategy, it is appropriate to determine what you have going for you in the change effort (supporting forces) and what you have going against you (restraining forces).

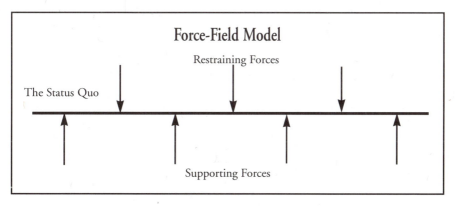

Figure 12.3.
A model for reducing resistance to change.

What the force-field model suggests is that the process of introducing change is highly political. Getting as many people onboard in support of the changes is only part of the strategy. It is also important to identify the sources of resistance and bring about a *reduction* of these forces. Many executives make the mistake of thinking that people will automatically support changes that appear good for the business. A detailed force-field analysis allows the management team to develop a strategy that minimizes the influence of the resistance forces.

STRATEGY 9. COMMUNICATE THE MESSAGE: "THERE WILL BE NO TURNING BACK!"

Everyone in the organization must believe that RapidResponse management is not another passing fad, but an irreversible change in the way the organization will be managed. Any kind of second-guessing on the part of management will telegraph the wrong message to employees: People have an easier time coping with change when the options are spelled out clearly.

STRATEGY 10. REEDUCATE THE "MIDDLES"

A discussion of the changes that need to be made by middle management as RapidResponse management practices are introduced was presented in Chapter Nine. It was suggested that the middle-level managers would need to abandon "direct-and-control" management in favor of a new role that emphasized leadership and coordination. Because these managers are so critical to the success of RapidResponse management, a discussion of the reeducation process is appropriate.

Managers have carried the baggage of being associated with behaviors of control, direction, and knowing what is best for others. Traditionally, these managers have been preoccupied with prescription. A key step in creating the RapidResponse enterprise is getting managers to let go of the idea that someone needs to be in control of the process. As Peter Block has eloquently stated, there needs to be a partnering between managers and workers rather than patriarchy. We have almost 200 years of experience telling us that patriarchy will not instill a sense of ownership and responsibility.

To create an organization that can respond quickly and responsibly requires a different type of governance—it calls for a service orientation rather than a control orientation. The focus is on a partnership between management and employees to make things happen for the benefit of the total enterprise. Managers are more oriented to winning in the marketplace than to promoting their own departmental interests.

The management class was once justified on the basis of the need for more control, consistency, and predictability. However, a strong class structure makes an organization incapable of offering real service. The more levels in the organization, the slower the response time. The more watching and inspecting, the less responsibility people need to take for the quality of their work. This is not to suggest that a hierarchy should be completely eliminated. In my view, hierarchy should be as flat and as small as possible. There is, of course, a need for someone at the top to define the purpose of the business. But changes having to do with customer service, quality, and cycle time require ownership and responsibility on the part of the front-line employees and the middle-level managers. The people at the top serve as brokers, providing the resources.

No one should be able to make a living simply planning, watching, controlling, or evaluating the actions of others.

Peter Block, author,
Stewardship: Choosing Service over Self-interest

Change does not need to be controlled by top management. Most employees, including middle managers, do not respond favorably to behavior that is perceived as overly directive or manipulative. The kind of change that needs to take place comes form *within* individuals, and this cannot be dictated by top management. By the same token, middle-level managers and supervisors can't dictate change to front-line employees. The problem is that management, because of years of conditioning, can easily slip into the parenting role, deciding what is best for employees. When management tries to make everyone do business process reengineering or total quality management, they are in the *control* paradigm. Empowerment does not come from the top; it means creating an environment where individuals can act with ownership and responsibility. Ideally, *everyone* needs to be involved in creating corporate vision and culture. The blitz change strategy, pioneered by Deevy Gilligan International and described in Chapter Ten, provides a process for gaining this organizationwide involvement.

Will there be a need for managers and supervisors in the future? It seems clear that management personnel will play a different role in high-performance work organizations. With the shift from a vertical division of labor to a horizontal division, managers/supervisors will be responsible for coordinating the activities of the various groups involved in delivering products or services to customers. They will be responsible for making everyone in the process feel they are playing a meaningful role.

As already indicated in Chapter Nine, the "middles" will need to undergo a major reorientation to assume the new coordinating role. They will need to undergo a reeducation that results in a change in mind-set and behaviors. We have found that intensive off-site management retreats are the most effective and efficient way of helping middle-level managers embrace the "new thinking."

STRATEGY 11. USE THE SERVICES OF A GUIDE

The pioneering Americans who traveled West on the wagon trains used guides to scout out the terrain and to warn of impending dangers. The organization going through change can benefit from the services of an outside expert who understands the dynamics of organizational behavior. This guide serves as a sounding board for management and helps them orchestrate the change process. A highly skilled and experienced organizational consultant can play an invaluable role in helping management negotiate through the various stages of the transformation process. Unfortunately, with the dramatic increase in the number of individuals claiming to be "organizational consultants," it has become more difficult to identify those who have the needed expertise.

What to Look For in a Consultant

The external consultant plays a critical role in helping a company navigate its way through the change process. Individuals who specialize in helping companies undergo a cultural transformation are referred to as organizational development (OD) consultants. While the marketplace has an abundance of people who classify themselves as management consultants, not all of these consultants have OD skills.

Common-sense considerations to keep in mind in selecting a consultant include the following:

- Put a priority on *experience*. The dynamics of organizational change can be extremely complex. Guiding an organization through a cultural change is not a job for amateurs.
- Steer clear of consultants who are primarily interested in selling a prepackaged product. Usually the only thing that is customized is the covers on the workbooks!
- While a strong background in the behavioral sciences is not an absolute requirement it is highly desirable.
- Pay attention to the "chemistry." The OD consultant becomes the therapist to the organization. The ability to create a trusting relationship is an indispensable requirement.
- Consider using a male-female consulting team. Both perspectives are important.
- The individual should have a high degree of integrity. Employees will quickly recognize someone who is just a "yes man" for management.
- Experienced OD consultants understand that successful change efforts are driven from *within* the company. The external consultant is a guide, not a driver.

Strategy # 12. Show Constancy of Purpose

Beware of the quick fix syndrome! Top management must show constancy of purpose and be willing to stick with the effort, especially when resistance is encountered. Ordinarily, a realistic time frame for bringing about a cultural change is one to three years. However, some changes can be instituted immediately. For example, establishing a program for sharing business information with employees can be introduced simply be scheduling town meetings and teaching employees how to interpret financial statements. Restructuring of the compensation system, on the other hand, requires considerable study. While the effort to streamline key processes can be started with very little advanced training, it ordinarily takes six months to a year to produce significant results. The key is for management to stay focused and to understand that the goal is to build a high-performance market-focused enterprise. Many employees have already become highly cynical of management initiatives to improve organizational performance. At this stage the "burden of proof" rests with top management.

THE CULTURAL TRANSFORMATION
HAS ALREADY BEGUN

The good news is that the "unfreezing" and accompanying revitalization of long-established businesses has already begun. There have been a variety of initiatives designed to make organizational structures more adaptive to the new business environment. *Powerful marketplace forces are now driving the effort to make businesses more competitive.* The motivation for changing management practices comes from a Darwinian need to survive and stay competitive. The changes now taking place reflect clearly identifiable trends in the workplace. These trends include

- Moving the work force closer to the customer
- Giving the individual employee authority to do more for the customer without asking the permission of management

- Shortening the decision chain

These trends can be found in the most progressive companies. The intent is to make the employee accountable for the work he or she is responsible for performing, with the authority to do everything possible to assure speedy delivery of a quality product or service. Obviously, these characteristics are not found in traditional hierarchical organizations.

Some companies are attempting to deal with the problems with hierarchies by moving toward high-performance teams. This structure uses a team to perform a process that is made up of as few as 5 members and as many as 40 members. They may or may not have a manager in the team. If not, the structure is called a *self-managing team*, although it will report to a manager who is not a member. One critical aspect of this structure is that the team must receive part of its compensation as a pool to be shared among members. The amount of the pool is calculated on the basis of what the team contributes to the business. As indicated in Chapter Six, operationalizing this concept requires considerable research.

There is a sharp contrast between working on a self-managed team and working in a traditional hierarchical organization. The self-managed team is charged with a particular area of work, but the members decide among themselves how to do the work and how to assign it. The compensation system reinforces the idea of completing the task in the fastest and most efficient manner possible. Typically, the self-managed teams run like little businesses within a business.

The move toward greater individual accountability for customer service and toward increased use of teams gives only two indications that the old management culture is changing. Other changes that reflect the move away form the traditional bureaucratic paradigm include the following:

1. *Breaking down of class distinctions.* An emerging awareness that everyone needs management skills is breaking down the historical boundary between a decision-making and a working class.

When workers perform management tasks for themselves, cycle time is reduced and customer service enhanced. As Peter Block says, it no longer makes sense to have people in the organization who make a living simply by watching and correcting the behavior of others.

2. *Redesign of individual jobs.* There is an increasing awareness that a *team approach,* focused on addressing the needs of the customer, can be more effective than the traditional emphasis on narrowly defined jobs.

3. *Redefining of staff groups.* A new understanding of the role of staff groups, such as human resources or finance, is emerging. In the new market-oriented business environment these groups are seen as resources or consultants to the people directly involved in serving the customer.

4. *Creating practices and policies that support the people who produce.* Various practices, such as performance appraisal, are being redesigned to better serve the needs of employees. A few organizations have taken the plunge and replaced the personnel manual with a simple list of guidelines.

5. *Redesigning the reward system.* As already indicated, companies are realizing that increased responsibility must be accompanied by increased compensation. Pay for skills and gain sharing is just the beginning; all employees need to realize their pay is related to the economic consequences of their efforts. The pay structure for all levels should be related to real business outcomes. The people who are responsible for the profits need to share in the gains. Company directors must realize that profit-making organizations do not exist only for the economic benefit of those who invest money in company stock, but also for those who are investing their energies and skills.

In summary, the pressures of the marketplace are leading to a questioning of traditional practices. The cultural transformation is already underway. Some companies have progressed more than others in the process of "reinventing" themselves.

GETTING STARTED
—THE LEADERSHIP CHALLENGE

Whether management use the five-stage blitz change model or a customized change strategy, the most challenging step is selling people at every level on the new ideas. The question is sometimes asked: "Do we start at the top or at the bottom?" The answer is that *change should be initiated at all levels*. It is essential that people throughout the organization develop ownership for the new ideas and a commitment to successful implementation. Management must do a good job of selling the need for change to employees.

Before getting started there are several questions that the leader should ask:

1. Do I *really want* these changes? Ambivalence on the part of the leader will cause people to sit on the fence.

2. Is there a *critical mass* of people who share my insights, vision, and commitment to change? Too many leaders go charging forward without making sure that they have the support of the work force.

3. Is my management information system providing me with accurate information on what is happening in the business? There is always a danger that the executive at the top will be isolated from what people down in the organization are really thinking and feeling.

4. Do we have systems, processes, and structures that will allow change to continue progressing toward the goal that we desire? The leader needs to know that there is an infrastructure in place that will carry the change process forward.

5. Do I have internal and/or external expertise to help guide the process? Most executives have limited experience in the field of organizational psychology.

The role of the person at the top is not to make change happen but to point people in the right direction. Executives need to resist the temptation to micromanage the change process.

The biggest challenge is getting started. Once the initial barriers are overcome, the process can move forward smoothly. The sentiments of one executive are worth keeping in mind: "If I had to do it again I would do it *sooner* and *faster* . . . it has so many benefits once you get over the *terrible hurdle* of getting started."

EMPLOYEES MUST ADAPT TO CHANGE

The focus on organizational change strategies, as outlined in this chapter, must be combined with an effort to help individuals adapt to the new environment. How to help employees develop the flexibility and versatility needed in the RapidResponse environment will be explored in the following chapter.

Management must be able to identify those who are highly adaptable to lead the change effort. In addition, they must help those imbued with a bureaucratic mind-set adjust to an environment that places a high priority on flexibility and versatility. The paradigm shift described in this book requires that employees go from an environment that favored structure and predictability to an environment that favors continuous adaptation. The new environment demands resilience on the part of employees. The question of how to build resilience and promote adaptability is a critical issue and deserves further exploration.

Creating the Resilient Organization:
Lesson 12

A traditional bureaucratic work organization cannot be converted into a highly responsive and resilient enterprise without a transformation of the old culture. In addition to the blitz strategy with its potential for sudden change, we now have a better understanding of the dynamics involved in letting go of the past and embracing the future.

CHAPTER 13

BUILDING SUPPORT FOR CHANGE:
Identify Your Resilient Employees

"All politics are local." This is the way the late Speaker of the U.S. Congress, Thomas "Tip" O'Neill, summed up his political philosophy. In a like manner, my motto is: "All organizational change is *personal.*" In earlier chapters I have described in detail the challenge involved in getting organizations to change the way they do business. However, the successful introduction of new practices into any organization ultimately depends on the ability of *individuals* to respond with flexibility and versatility to changes. In this chapter we will explore how the adaptability of employees can be increased. To be effective, people must be able to move at the pace of change.

In 1985, Deevy Gilligan International was established as a research and development firm with a primary focus on *organizational* change. Our focus on organizations necessitated research on how individuals within the organization adapt to change. This research became a central focus of DGI and led us to develop a methodology for assessing the adaptability of managers and employees. We began to use tools that would help pinpoint where training and development resources should be concentrated.

Prior to conducting this research, during my tenure as a faculty member in organizational psychology at a major university in Massachusetts, I had begun to study the question of why some individuals are more adaptive than others. I did not consider the issue of adaptability to be merely theoretical; indeed, I first began to contemplate the issue when I discovered that my own colleagues at the university—tenured professors—were traumatized when confronted with change in their expectations. Because as individuals the majority were not stress resilient, the entire group of professors began to behave in a highly dysfunctional manner.

At DGI, I began to analyze the behavior of my former colleagues and others like them—people who broke down under the stress of change. With my associates, I carried out research and collected data in a way frequently used by cultural anthropologists. First, we observed people in many different work environments. Those observed included teachers, scientists, bankers, factory operators, nurses, physicians, and engineers. Some less conventional groups such as the members of a 500-year-old religious community of women were also part of our research. When we analyzed our data, we found patterns in the way individuals respond when confronted with disruptions in their expectations. A high percentage responded with fear and defensiveness, but there were others whose behavior remained stable and steady while under pressure, and still others whose behavior became energetic, almost animated.

An oversimplified but powerful conclusion from our research can be stated as follows: *The rate at which normal people can be expected to assimilate change will vary from person to person.* A type that we might call the resilient person has the capacity to absorb high levels of change while displaying minimal dysfunctional behaviors. This resiliency level does not correlate with age or educational level. The amount of stress exhibited by the individual in the face of unexpected disruptions correlates more with *length of time* and personal values. Different types of people can tolerate change/disruption for different periods of time. The time expands if a person's passion, beliefs, and value-needs are being met during the disruption.

FUTURE SHOCK HAS ARRIVED

In 1970 Alvin Toffler introduced the concept of "future shock" with the publication of his book predicting the debilitating effects of major changes on the individual. Future shock is the stress induced in individuals when they are subjected to too much change. In work with various organizations both in the United States and in Europe, we at DGI have observed that future shock has already arrived in the marketplace: The pace of change has accelerated to the point that the environment is changing faster than the ability of many people to adapt. Increasingly, we see workers who are overwhelmed by the changes taking place around them and are suffering from overload. When individuals exceed their absorption threshold, they begin to display signs of dysfunction—poor judgment, short-term memory loss, job dissatisfaction, fatigue, emotional burnout, feelings of inadequacy and cyclical, mild illness.

When introducing the RapidResponse model, we are often asked to identify those people in organizations who could most effectively champion the new paradigm. Recognizing at an early stage that adaptability is a key ingredient for success in an environment where the only constant is change, we asked ourselves how we could separate those individuals who were flexible and versatile from those who experienced psychological barriers to change.

DGI cofounder Kathleen Gilligan began to address this question through use of a behavioral assessment instrument called the *Style Analysis*. This instrument, by providing a mechanism for measuring adaptability, proved to be a major enhancement of our efforts at transforming work organizations. We soon discovered that Style Analysis could provide a complete profile of the organizations' "adaptability-to-change" potential by allowing us to predict the ability of managers and employees to adapt to the RapidResponse environment.

Furthermore, Style Analysis provided a base line for designing programs to increase the resiliency level of employees.

DISC INSTRUMENT:
A BEHAVIORAL SNAPSHOT

The Style Analysis is more widely known by its generic name—the DISC instrument. It measures four observable behavioral traits that were first identified by William Moulton Marston, a Harvard-educated psychologist whose work was first published in the 1920s. An assessment instrument based on Marston's work was first introduced in the 1960s; the version of the DISC instrument used by DGI was developed in the 1980s by Bill Bonnstetter and his colleagues at Target Training International in Scottsdale, Arizona. In recent years Bonnstetter has pioneered the development of various computerized applications of the DISC instrument.

What You Should Know About Tests

Here are a few things to consider before using any test in your organization:

- *Not all tests are reliable.* Some are of little more value than the horoscope in the morning newspaper. Unfortunately, it is a seller's market with very little protection for the customer. The group that has historically evaluated test instruments is the American Psychological Association. However, many of the commonly used workplace tests have not yet received APA evaluation.

- *Instruments designed to measure behavioral traits or personality preferences can be misused.* An example of a serious misuse is the labeling or "typing" of individuals. This is often the result of failing to understand the moderating or enegizing effect that combinations of behavioral traits have on each other. Describing a manager or an employee as a "high C" or as an "ENTP" reflects an amateurish and unprofessional use of assessment instruments. The use of instruments is serious business. They are not ice-breakers or the subject of cocktail party chitchat.

- *The results from tests such as the Style Analysis or the Myers-Briggs Type Indicator (MBTI) should be interpreted by an individual with a solid background in the behavioral sciences or in-depth training on the theory and application of the specific instrument.* The use of these instruments by untrained individuals is as inappropriate as having a layperson interpret the results of an MRI or an X ray. Appropriate time must be given to understanding the correlation of various behavioral factors and how they are impacted by workplace environment.

- *Some of the more widely used instruments, such as the MBTI, have training materials and training programs for users.* One of several books describing the Style Analysis is *DISC: A Reference Manual* by Bill Bonnstetter, Judy Suiter, and Randy Jay Widrick (Scottsdale, AZ: Target Training International,1993). Kathleen Gilligan, a cofounder of DGI, specializes in providing professional consultation on the use of the Style Analysis as a tool for supporting organizational transformation (Telephone: 508/688-4900, fax: 508/975-7691).

The Style Analysis is the psychological equivalent of a Polaroid instant photo. It analyzes behavioral style, that is, a person's manner of doing things. In the DISC method, a questionnaire is used to generate data on an individual's intensity level of dominance, influence, steadiness, and compliance. The questionnaire ordinarily requires 7 to 10 minutes to complete, and can be obtained by using the Response Form in the back of the book. The data from the questionnaire are plotted on two computer-generated graphs, one that demonstrates the real or basic style and the other that interprets behavior an individual believes must be projected to achieve success in a given environment. A reading is provided on the intensity level of the individual on each of four key behavioral traits. The report generated by this instrument provides a double exposure snapshot. We see a person's preferred work style and also get to see how the individual perceives, and adapts to, their present environment.

The Style Analysis instrument does *not* measure personality or abnormal behavior. It is an *educational* tool that provides easy-to-understand information on observable behavior. Therefore, what we get from the Style Analysis is a portrait of normal behavior and an adaptability reading. Though people are much more complex than the model shows, the information generated by the Style Analysis is invaluable in predicting how an individual may be expected to act in a new environment.

What follows is a brief description of each of the four measured traits. This is not intended as a detailed analysis but simply a capsule description of the high side of each factor. The instrument generates an abundance of data: Over 350 graphs can be plotted from the responses.

D = DOMINANCE

How a person approaches problems and deals with challenges. Words that can be used to describe the behavior of a person whose highest scores are on the D factor include forceful, dominant, decisive, results oriented, impatient, demanding, competitive, bold, authoritative, strong willed, and aggressive. Many of the entrepreneurs we have profiled over the past five years exhibit high dominance (D). Since expediting action is often associated with a strong D factor, there is a good chance that this type of person would thrive in a RapidResponse environment. But the D is just one of four factors. Before a prediction can be made about resiliency level, it's necessary to look at dominance in relationship to the other three factors.

I = INFLUENCE

How a person interacts with, and attempts to influence, others. Words that can be used to describe a person whose highest score is on the I factor include enthusiastic, gregarious, persuasive, optimistic, impulsive, confident, sociable, talkative, generous, and open minded. There seems to be an innate optimism that emanates from people with a high I score. *We believe the I factor score is the best indicator of resiliency.*

S = STEADINESS

How a person responds to change and levels of activity. Words that can be used to describe the high S trait include steady, predictable, systematic, understanding, passive, possessive, serene, sincere, and stable. A high S factor is indicative of patience, persistence, and a preference for tradition and harmony. It is estimated that about 40% of the population have a preference for high S behavior. Having to juggle many balls at once is stressful for the high S individual; he or she prefers a stable and predictable environment. The person with the strong S trait tends to resist what he or she perceives as unnecessary change. Although he or she most often exhibits a calm, steady, outward appearance, this person will experience the introduction of Rapid-Response concepts as chaotic and therefore stressful.

C = COMPLIANCE

How the individual responds to rules and procedures set by others. Words that describe a person who's highest score is on the C factor include conscientious, precise, systematic, analytical, conventional, sensitive, perfectionistic, mature, and restrained. The high C person, with a preference for precise procedures, may initially lack the flexibility needed in the RapidResponse environment; he or she can be expected to react negatively to sudden and unexpected changes and may suffer from "paralysis by analysis." More than anything else, high C behavior reflects a need for accuracy and a fear of criticism. Clearly, this can lead to stress in an environment that demands continuous change and a departure from the familiar.

ALL ARE NOT EQUALLY ADAPTABLE

There is no "good" or "bad" when it comes to interpreting a person's Style Analysis graph. The intensity level on each of the four traits will vary from one person to another, and different styles tend to complement each other in the workplace: The person with the high S will provide stability while the person with the high I will create the enthusiasm essential for any high-performance group; the high C will provide the rational analysis, while the high D will provide the drive needed to overcome obstacles. The ideal organization has individuals with all four styles. However, in today's dynamic changing environment, with its need for increased responsiveness to the marketplace, a profile that shows low or moderate levels of S and C, combined with a higher I, is a good predictor of resiliency.

Research conducted by Bonnstetter and others suggests that over the past few decades there has been gradual adaptation of workers toward what I have described as the RapidResponse environment. In 1979, 55% of the managers in Bonnstetter's study were high on the S factor. By 1993, this number had decreased to 40%. Conversely, there were only 15% who tested high on the I factor in 1979. This has now risen to 28%. There was no significant change on the D or C factors. These statistics are very heartening. People can and do change. Later in this chapter I offer specific suggestions for facilitating change and adaptation.

The following observations should be kept in mind when using the Style Analysis as a tool for assessing the readiness of the organization for change.

- The employee with a basic style that is high D or high I will be comfortable working in an organization that operates according to RapidResponse principles. It is helpful to have some people with these profiles when it comes time to make major changes. In mature companies, it is sometimes necessary to "import" several high D's and high I's to champion the new way of doing business.
- Individuals whose highest scores are on the S or C factor will be less inclined to lead the way when major changes in the way the

company operates are introduced. The more radical the change, the more stress and discomfort.

- In using the Style Analysis over a five-year period, we have found that nearly 60% of employees in older established organizations exhibit high S and high C behavior. The implications of this finding are obvious for any executive attempting to change the culture of his or her organization. It means that a majority of workers are *naturally inclined* to resist change to maintain the status quo.

- The Style Analysis instrument is a highly efficient way of identifying individuals and groups who need resiliency training and support.

WHAT MAKES PEOPLE *ADAPTABLE?*

Use of the Style Analysis confirms my early observations about the varying levels of adaptability that can be found in any work group. At DGI, we had always found, when implementing RapidResponse principles, that some individuals experience more difficulty than others in absorbing change.

While much remains unknown about the complex factors affecting the ability of employees to adapt to sudden or unexpected changes, I can offer these tentative conclusions:

1. The ability of the individual to adapt to the environment is a critical condition for success in the modern business environment.

2. Adaptability can be divided into two basic components—flexibility and versatility. The word *flexibility* refers to an attitude we have toward change, and *versatility* has to do with our competencies or abilities for dealing with new situations.

3. In general, people view themselves as more flexible and versatile than they actually are. There is a gap between our idealized and our actual level of adaptability.

4. Higher *flexibility* is characterized by a number of personal characteristics, including

- Positive outlook—flexible people see the glass as half-full and getting fuller
- Open-mindedness
- Confidence in one's self
- Sensitivity toward others

5. *Versatility* involves a set of personal aptitudes that goes beyond being willing to adapt. Versatility is a complex set of mental and emotional abilities that we acquire over time through a variety of resources. More versatile people approach every situation in each day of their lives as new opportunities for learning and growing.

6. Higher *versatility* is characterized by several personal aptitudes, including:

- Vision and imagination
- Resourcefulness—from "we can do it" to "this too shall pass"
- Ability to learn from feedback
- Attentiveness to environment
- Lifelong learning

EVEN HARDHEADS CAN CHANGE!

Work with diverse client organizations throughout the North American continent and abroad has led us to one very welcome conclusion: Individual managers and employees *can* increase their flexibility and versatility.

When the telephone industry was first deregulated by the federal government, employees experienced a form of "future shock." They had been operating in a hothouse environment—insulated from the competitive pressures of the marketplace—and some found it so difficult to adjust to new realities that they became known as "bell-heads."

Workplace Resiliency

Webster's *New Collegiate Dictionary* defines the word resiliency as "an ability to recover from or adjust easily to misfortune or change." When William Safire was asked to sum up the life of the late President Nixon in one word on *Meet the Press,* he used the word *resilient.* In the political arena Nixon acquired the reputation of an individual who would constantly fight back after setbacks.

The concept of resilience is very useful in thinking about the kind of person who is likely to be successful in the RapidResponse work environment. Here are the characteristics you are likely to find in a resilient employee:

1. *Positive attitude.* They understand that things are not always going to go right but they believe in their ability to be successful.

2. *Proactive behavior.* They don't sit around waiting for something to happen. Work is not merely something to be endured: They take satisfaction in having a sense of control and acting accordingly.

3. *Vision and focus.* The resilient person doesn't waste energy spinning his or her wheels. There is a sense of direction and a focus to activity.

4. *Ability to tolerate ambiguity.* Resilient people can live with uncertainty. They know it is normal, and all right, not to have the answers.

5. *Strong organizational skills.* They have the ability to "make sense" out of chaos.

6. *Ability to pick themselves up and carry on.*

Every mature company has a significant number of "hardheads"—people who see change as something that is physiologically impossible. Our experience is that even the most hard-headed types can be assisted in adapting to new realities if the proper techniques are used.

As discussed earlier, individuals in any company or institution display a wide variation in their ability to adapt. To maintain a RapidResponse environment, special attention should be given to those who, for whatever reasons, are most inflexible and lacking in versatility.

There is no one-size-fits-all formula for increasing individual adaptability. The starting point in every case, however, should be the establishment of a behavioral base line using the Style Analysis or some other effective assessment tool. Then, the effort to help the individual cope with change can be combined and integrated with the broader strategies for creating a RapidResponse environment that were described in earlier chapters.

EIGHT TECHNIQUES TO HELP EMPLOYEES ADAPT

A customized program for helping managers and employees adapt to the fast-changing RapidResponse environment can be developed using a combination of the following techniques:

1. Induce pain and provide a reward.

There is a story told about an oil rigger who survived a disastrous fire on one of the North Sea oil platforms. When asked in an interview after the accident if it had been difficult for him to decide to jump into such perilous waters, the rigger responded that the *possibility* of survival was much more attractive than the certainty of death on the burning rig. To help employees adapt, managers must orchestrate pain messages throughout the organization as a way of gaining commitment to the change. The state-of-the-company monthly meetings, described in Chapter Six, provide the ideal forum for communicating these messages. However, while management points out the grim alternatives, they must also allow employees the freedom to positively impact their future.

2. Provide coaching/mentoring for managers.

Many managers who are unable to make the paradigm shift end up in the offices of the outplacement firm. Unfortunately, these firms show little interest in helping the individual look at behavioral traits that may have caused them to be fired in the first place. The result is that individuals frequently become part of a revolving door as they continue to have difficulty adapting to the environment.

Some managers and employees need psychological counseling if they are to make the adjustments needed to be successful in the new work environment. A growing number of progressive companies now provide professional coaching for key managers, an investment in human resources that makes a lot of sense. The coach should be a professional in the behavioral sciences who has an understanding of the dynamics of the business environment. Mentoring is also an overlooked but extremely valuable tool in helping the change process.

3. Reduce blind spots.

Feedback can be provided in conjunction with the professional coaching described earlier. Several good instruments are available that have been designed to get feedback from peers, subordinates, and superiors. Sometimes referred to as 360-degree feedback, this input from a variety of sources provides a powerful mechanism for encouraging the individual to make needed changes.

4. Let people know that they will either be architects or the victims of change; there is no other choice.

In earlier chapters I stressed the need to provide employees with business information: The more people know about what is going on, the less likely they are to feel out of control. In addition, training and development designed to increase an internal locus of control will contribute to helping employees overcome feelings of victimization.

Resources to Consider

From the many psychological instruments available for generating data on personal behavior I recommend two in particular. The *16PF*, as the name suggests, measures sixteen personality factors. The profile generated by the *16PF* is very useful when personality issues are involved. This instrument is available only through a qualified psychologist.

The Center for Creative Leadership, an independent, non-profit educational institution in North Carolina, developed *Skillscope* as a means of generating 360 degree feedback for middle managers and first-line supervisors and *Benchmarks* for providing feedback to executives. The assessment includes feedback from peers and subordinates. The Center also offers off-site leadership training for executives.

---

5. Provide employees with an understanding of the dynamics of the change process.

The painful process of coping with disrupted expectations follows certain predictable stages. Providing a framework for understanding what is happening can help reduce fears and anxieties. In Chapter Twelve, I used the three-stage model developed by William Bridges as a way of explaining organizational change. This model can also be used to explain the psychodynamics of personal change.

6. Encourage people to question their assumptions.

An attitude that communicates the "not-invented-here" message can be fatal. The willingness to openly question existing assumptions needs to be part of the new culture. The organization must provide rewards for innovation and risk taking.

7. Offer workshops on creativity.

Employees need to be encouraged to engage in right-brain activity. This training can compensate for the past failure of the educational system to foster creative thinking in students. It can also role model the preferred behaviors associated with right-brain thinking—a benefit that will be appreciated by cautious employees.

8. Create a perpetual learning environment.

The need to promote continuous learning will be discussed in detail in Chapter Fourteen. When major changes are implemented we recommend the creation of discussion groups to allow employees to process their feelings.

BARRIERS TO INCREASING EMPLOYEE ADAPTABILITY

Some things that get in the way of promoting employee flexibility and versatility are

- *Red tape.* The organization becomes so bureaucratic that people are no longer able to see their own myopic behavior.
- *Past success.* People believe that a history of accomplishment in the past is somehow a guarantee for the future.
- *An arrogant attitude.* It is difficult to get people to consider new possibilities if there is a prevailing "we know it all" culture.
- *Fear of unemployment.* The fear of negative consequences can be a powerful force in keeping an individual from changing.
- *Human nature.* This is the biggest obstacle to change. Humans have a natural tendency to resist change.

CHANGE: DANGER OR OPPORTUNITY

When an organization is going through change, it is often in a state of crisis. The relation between change and crisis has long been recognized: The Chinese *define* change as a time of crisis. In the Chinese language, the symbol for crisis represents both *danger* and *hidden opportunity.* When we are feeling tired or stressed we are more likely to focus on the danger. We know this from personal experience. For example, while writing this book I experienced some unexpected changes in my business life. At first these changes caused considerable anxiety. Later, however, I was able to see the new opportunities. Thus, these changes reaffirmed for me something that I have known for a long time: *The anticipation of change is always more anxiety producing than the actual change itself.*

As we encounter the unexpected we invariably find that change does indeed present *opportunity*. What makes change difficult is that the opportunity is not on our radar screen. It is *hidden* opportunity.

In implementing the RapidResponse concepts described in this book, it is important not to lose sight of the emotional difficulty that people experience when they are asked to make changes. Don't lose patience with the "hardheads." These employees don't need a manager with a 2 by 4 who is trying to bully them into accepting the new ideas; even the most inflexible employees are willing to take risks and step into the deep water if they know that there is an outreached hand that will assist them in getting to the other side. Patience and persistence are therefore required; understanding and respecting psychological differences are an important part of getting people to make changes. Often, when initially fearful employees do get with the program there is no stopping them! Let your naturally optimistic, self-confident high I, low C employees lead the way. Be sure to mentor the others or your advance guard will find they have no one charging up the hill behing them.

BUILDING THE INTELLIGENT WORK ORGANIZATION

Promoting flexibility and versatility in the workplace requires a work environment where people are continually exposed to new ideas. In the old bureaucratic work environment, characterized by stability and predictability, employee education was a low priority. Working in the RapidResponse mode requires a culture that supports perpetual learning and innovation. To a large extent, the ability to compete successfully is based on the ability to capitalize on the organization's intelligence. How to create an environment that promotes constant innovation will be explored in the following chapter.

Creating the Resilient Organization: Lesson 13

The high-performance organization of the future will be inhabited by *resilient employees*. Those employees who are most resilient can play a key role in leading the transformation. Having the ability to measure employee resiliency is a major asset in a strategy for creating the resilient workplace.

C H A P T E R 1 4

PROMOTING INNOVATION AND CREATIVITY:
Create a Learning Culture

"We are so busy making changes that we don't have time for business" is the way one middle manager expressed her frustration. What she did not understand is that there is no going back to "business as usual." In a continually changing marketplace, the competitive business organization must be capable of managing the transformation process while at the same time paying close attention to business. The challenge confronting management is to learn how to foster a dynamic learning environment while keeping people sharply focused on the bottom line. This means that the business enterprise must evolve into a "learning organization."

RapidResponse management provides the *foundation* for building the high-performance enterprise. However, introducing these new management practices is only a beginning. Maintaining competitiveness requires continuous adaptation. The challenge is to avoid hardening of the bureaucratic arteries. The successful business enterprise must have the ability to continuously respond to an ever-changing marketplace. As my colleague Daniel Tobin has pointed out (Oliver

Wight, VT: *Reeducating the Corporation: Foundations for the Learning Organization*, 1994), continuous change demands an unrelenting commitment to continuous learning.

Any business that wants to maintain the competitive edge must place a high priority on operating in the learning mode. The company that does not understand the need for a constant infusion of new ideas is in serious trouble. As discussed in Chapter Eleven, a company can become a victim of *paradigm paralysis*.

> **Continuous change demands an unrelenting commitment to learning.**

The concept of the learning organization, despite its wide acceptance in recent years, is rarely understood in management circles. Part of the problem is that the concept seems to lack "flesh and bones"—it seems too esoteric. Proponents fail to specify in concrete terms what they mean by a learning organization.

THE LEARNING ORGANIZATION

The most successful companies of the 1990s will be *learning* organizations. These are adaptive enterprises where workers are free to think for themselves, to identify problems and opportunities, and to go after them. In the learning organization people share a passion for personal and corporate improvement. People feel a sense of responsibility to learn how to do things better and are proactive in seeking ways to improve what they do. The person who is willing to question the old assumptions is admired. There is a curiosity about what other companies are doing. The idea that "if it ain't broke, don't fix it" is rejected. The need to constantly improve work processes and systems is accepted as standard operating procedure. The organization is constantly studying itself and its marketplace. Everyone, from CEO to front-line worker, is constantly striving to improve his or her skills. Learning becomes an integral part of the work environment.

FOSTERING A LEARNING CULTURE: FIVE STEPS

There is no cookbook formula for creating a work environment where there is openness to new ideas and a commitment to continuous learning. Clearly, the example of the people at the top can have a major impact. If top managers show a curiosity for learning new ideas and developing new skills, this will have a ripple effect throughout the company.

The process of creating the learning organization can be reduced to five general steps. These steps provide a broad framework for considering how a learning culture can be fostered.

STEP 1. USE VISION AS THE CONTEXT FOR LEARNING.

Once the vision for the future is articulated, it is easy to decide what learning needs to take place. Learning is focused on developing the knowledge and skills needed to work toward making the vision a reality. The process of becoming a learning organization will vary from company to company. A business enterprise that is moving into foreign markets will need language training for some of its people. Likewise, a hospital involved in moving into the outpatient services market may need to have some employees develop marketing skills. In certain cases the need will be for basic skills such as math or English-as-a-second-language. In every situation the focus is on developing the skills needed to work toward the vision for the future.

As indicated earlier, leaders must clearly define and communicate the vision. Once the direction of the company is clearly established it is relatively easy to identify the learning that needs to be undertaken. Useful questions to ask in developing a program of learning include

1. *What factors will be important to the success of the company over the next two to three years?* The leaders must be able to look into the future and get a clear picture of what the business climate will be like and how the company will fit in. They must be able

to identify the knowledge and skills needed to maintain competitiveness. The ability to anticipate the skills that will be needed in the future is a very important management skill.

2. *Are there technological trends that can put the company in a better position than competitors?* An awareness of what is happening on the technological front has become a condition for survival. Again, the ability to anticipate the technological skills needed in the future is essential.

3. *What initiatives can the company take, such as reducing cycle time, that can give you a competitive advantage?* In a highly dynamic marketplace a company must maintain constant alertness for opportunities to reduce cost, increase quality, and increase speed to market.

4. *What steps might your competitor take to put your company at a disadvantage?* Understanding that a company has to be better than the competition is an important step on the road to maintaining the competitive edge. The importance of benchmarking against competitors cannot be overstated.

5. *Does your customer have an unmet need or unfilled expectations?* The answer to this question can only be found by reaching out to the marketplace. In a learning organization people are continually asking the question: What do they want from us?

These five questions need to be addressed within the context of the strategic objectives that have been established. As previously indicated, the vision sets the overall direction and management is continuously engaged in helping the organization find its niche in the marketplace. The whole organization must be constantly asking questions similar to the five listed above for learning to be relevant and useful in helping the company be successful in the marketplace.

STEP 2. DEVELOP A PLAN.

The larger vision for improvement must be turned into specific action steps. How you measure your progress depends on the plan itself.

Whether the overall goal includes reduced production time, a changing market focus or quality improvement, a detailed time line is necessary. Planning and a system of measurement keep the plan grounded in reality and prevent it from becoming an academic exercise. It also makes it easier to decide what learning is superfluous.

Many organizations fail to consider the kind of learning that is required in order to achieve their strategic objectives. For example, developing a customer-driven orientation will require a major reeducation of the work force for some companies. Likewise, a commitment to produce products of outstanding quality may require extensive training in statistical process control. What is needed in each case is an honest assessment of the learning needs of people throughout the organization. These needs must be translated into a plan that is achievable.

STEP 3. INSTITUTIONALIZE LEARNING.

Too many business leaders mistakenly think that by offering an occasional seminar or workshop they are creating a learning organization.

However, the most important learnings are derived from the experience of working in the organization itself. The work environment can be a lab where learning becomes an integral part of the work experience—not something added on. Information about the internal workings of the organization and the external environment in which the company operates is essential in maintaining the competitive edge. People need to learn about the work processes in which they work. They need assistance in adapting to the new technologies that are introduced. More important, they need to be continuously updated on the performance of the business in the marketplace. Learning that is divorced from the daily workplace experience is generally of little value.

Companies that ignore the learning needs of employees run the risk of becoming stale and losing competitiveness. To be uninformed about the internal workings of the company and the external marketplace is to be vulnerable to threats lurking outside the company and missed opportunities inside the company.

**The most important information that is communicated
in the learning organization is derived directly from the
experience of work.**

One of the characteristics of the true *learning organization* is that
people at every level are hungry for new ideas. Management want to
do whatever it takes to stay at the cutting edge. In the true learning
organization there is an open and fast flow of information.
Knowledge is what lubricates the company.

One of the themes throughout this book is the need to share
business information with employees at every level. The need for
employees to understand how the organization produces its goods or
services has been stressed. Likewise, the need for employees to understand how the organization stands in relation to the external marketplace has been emphasized. In work with client companies Deevy
Gilligan International has advocated a program of continuous learning that integrates information about the internal workings of the
business with information on what is happening in the marketplace.
The following comments are based on insights gained from working
with client companies.

1. Learning about the internal workings of the organization

The process of educating employees about the internal workings
of the company begins with the sharing of financial information. This
may require providing training so that employees can understand the
information that is presented. One way of institutionalizing the sharing of business information is through monthly state-of-the-business
meetings. As already indicated, employees also need to understand
how the business works. Helping employees identify and improve the
key business processes whereby the company delivers the service or
product to the market is an essential step in increasing this understanding.

The three tenets of RapidResponse management constitute the
core curriculum in the learning organization. However, there are
other opportunities to help employees increase knowledge and skills.

Feedback from employee surveys increases the level of awareness within the company. There are various ways of helping employees gain a deeper understanding of their own strengths and weaknesses. A variety of psychological instruments are available to help to increase self-understanding among managers and employees.

2. Learning about the external environment

What happens *outside* an organization often determines its success or failure. If internal achievements—no matter how great—don't meet the demands of the external environment, the results will be poor. Companies must interface with the rest of the world. Despite the obvious importance of external information, ideas that originate outside a company are the most underutilized source of knowledge. Key sources of information are customers and competitors.

In a learning organization the process of collecting information from the customer base is institutionalized. A structured approach to collecting information known as quality function deployment (QFD) was described in Chapter Ten. This methodology, pioneered in the Japanese auto industry, provides a means for staying in touch with the real needs and wants of customers. The information generated through the QFD process is communicated back to employees and contributes to the development of an educated work force.

In a learning organization *competitors* are also considered a major source of valuable information. A methodology for collecting this information known as benchmarking was referred to in Chapter Ten. Progressive companies are now using benchmarking as a means of comparing their performance with best-performing companies in the marketplace. Again, the information generated from this methodology is shared throughout the company and contributes to the development of a more educated work force.

The key idea is that learning is not left to chance. There are mechanisms that can be used to provide employees with input on what is happening inside the organization and in the external environment. In the learning organization these mechanisms become part of standard operating procedures. Learning becomes institutionalized.

STEP 4. PROMOTE CREATIVITY AND INNOVATION.

In addition to the institutionalized learning just described, the modern business organization also needs to foster creative activity. What is essential is that an environment that is conducive to creative problem solving be developed. Management must understand that good ideas can originate anywhere within the organization. We have found that creativity is more likely to flourish in an atmosphere that is free of fear and intimidation. Monetary rewards can be used effectively as a tool for promoting innovation and creativity.

> **Creativity is more likely to flourish in an atmosphere that is free of fear and intimidation.**

When it comes to solving problems, the most successful learning organizations spend little time trying to adapt old solutions to fit new problems. They face challenges with eyes open to fresh ideas and theories. They see problem solving as a real learning opportunity. New ideas and approaches can be threatening when a manager or company has invested heavily in old ideas that either have outlived their usefulness or never were particularly successful. The organization needs to make heroes out of the people who have the courage to question old assumptions.

Much of the training in the tools and techniques of total quality management and business process reengineering has done little to promote creativity and inventiveness. These approaches have tended to be overly mechanistic, with little emphasis on the importance of right-brain activity to the success of the enterprise. However, it is no longer enough to simply "do things right." *In the modern business environment the key is to do the right things.* The ability to question assumptions and reframe problems will be a key factor in staying competitive in the future.

STEP 5. FOSTER A PERPETUAL LEARNING CULTURE.

Implementing the suggestions put forward here requires a willingness to share information with people who formerly were excluded from the organization's database. It also requires a commitment from company management to the development of employees. Germany and Japan are examples of countries that have a much stronger tradition of committing company resources to the development of employees.

For many businesses, a commitment to employee development will represent a change in organizational culture. The learning needs of each company will vary. The 15 questions in Figure 14.1 provide a basis for assessing a company's learning needs. The key, as I have indicated, is that learning becomes part of the standard operating procedures. Learning becomes a continuous process that is institutionalized into the everyday life of the company. The program of learning will vary from company to company, depending on the needs that are identified. Most of the learning will be outside of formal classroom experiences. All of the learning will be designed to assist the company in achieving its strategic objectives.

The impetus for building the learning organization must come from the leaders at the top. The leadership has to be tenacious in overcoming resistance and in creating an environment that allows people to question assumptions. There has to be a belief that learning leads to new knowledge and that this knowledge is necessary for maintaining the competitive edge.

TRAINING MUST BE RELEVANT

American business organizations spend over $40 billion a year trying to develop their employees through formal training. However, most of this money, some $27 billion, is spent on only 0.5% of the 97 million who have full-time jobs. Even those companies that spend heavily on training often get very little return on the investment. Training is often presented in a sterile classroom setting and has very little impact on the work environment. Rarely is the training directly tied in to strategic objectives. Employees quickly learn that training is low on the list of management priorities.

As already indicated, the best learning comes from the actual work environment. Formal workshops and seminars have minimum impact on attitudes and behaviors. Employees are more likely to ben-

---

Learning Needs Checklist

This questionnaire is designed to surface areas to be addressed as part of the process of developing a learning organization:

1. We have a clear sense of direction (vision).   YES   NO
2. The vision is clearly communicated and understood by all.   YES   NO
3. Information on "the business of the business" is shared rapidly and widely.   YES   NO
4. The needs of "internal customers" are clearly understood.   YES   NO
5. The needs of clients/customers are clearly understood.   YES   NO
6. We understand the strengths and weaknesses of competitors.   YES   NO
7. We are kept up to date on the "financials."   YES   NO
8. Our customers provide feedback on our products or services.   YES   NO
9. We have skills needed to do a good job.   YES   NO
10. The training we do is actively supported by the work environment.   YES   NO
11. We are encouraged to take risks and try out new ideas.   YES   NO
12. We are open to "new thinking."   YES   NO
13. We are developing the technological expertise needed for tomorrow's marketplace.   YES   NO
14. Training in "the basics," such as math, is provided when needed.   YES   NO
15. Creativity, risk taking, and innovation are rewarded.   YES   NO
16. Employees are encouraged to increase their skills portfolio.   YES   NO

Figure 14.1.

efit from hands-on training provided by coworkers and supervisors. In the business world today, the focus is shifting from classroom teaching to on-the-job learning.

In their efforts to introduce Japanese management, some companies have invested heavily in teaching the tools and techniques of process improvement. The concepts presented are couched in jargon and unfamiliar language. In many cases, this technical training has no benefit because the workers have no immediate opportunities to put the new learnings into practice. Training can be considered a subset of learning, but it is not a substitute. For training to be effective employees must have the opportunity to use the new learning. Training should be communicated in language that is clearly comprehensible, and it should be relevant and add value by supporting the business strategy.

The best results can be found in companies where management are directly involved in providing the training. Managers who are inexperienced as trainers can partner with training specialists in conducting training sessions. The involvement of senior managers helps counteract the impression that employee development is a fringe activity.

BARRIERS TO CREATING A LEARNING CULTURE

The most serious barrier to organizational learning is an arrogant attitude that says "we already have the answers." When a company is enjoying success in the marketplace, it is more likely to succumb to this pernicious way of thinking. A history of success can blind a company to the need to question its own assumptions. Other factors that might contribute to poor results include

1. The failure to make a connection between the staff development program and the strategic business objectives of the company.
2. A "one-size-fits-all" approach is used. "Canned" staff development programs are generally a waste of time and resources.
3. The ideas presented in the classroom are sabotaged in the work situation by the manager.

4. Training is perceived as a fringe activity with little management support.

THE PAYOFF FOR CONTINUOUS LEARNING

Continuous learning makes it possible for the company to successfully cope with continuous change. In Chapter Eleven a disease called "paradigm blindness" was discussed. Unfortunately, many companies get stuck in a fixed mind-set, and the results are usually catastrophic. Knowledge derived from learning is the best antidote to paradigm paralysis. In a rapidly changing marketplace, companies can quickly become outdated. Wang Computer is just one of thousands of companies that fell on bad times because of the failure to continuously question cherished business assumptions. Like others, Wang was seduced into believing that past success would guarantee future success. And it is not just in high technology that companies have to be continuously learning. Hospitals, banks, retail stores—even educational institutions—are disappearing every day because of their inability to maintain the competitive edge. Without continuous learning an organization is not likely to survive in the current business climate. The payoff for promoting a learning organization is an environment where there is an increased capability for dealing with unplanned and unexpected changes in the marketplace.

In addition to increasing the ability of the company to cope with change, learning also promotes inventiveness and openness to new ideas. A program of continuous learning is a requirement for promoting innovation and creative solutions to problems. Learning also helps foster flexibility and responsiveness to the external environment. Increasingly, management are recognizing that open-mindedness among the work force is essential for success.

People who are learning are more open to improvement, change, and risk-taking. This is the kind of person we need.

John McDonnell,
Chairman, McDonnell Douglas

PROMOTING LEARNING:
EIGHT RECOMMENDATIONS

Management can promote learning in the organization by taking an active part in reeducation programs. Among the things that management can do are

1. *Identify gaps in the performance and capability of the organization.* The Learning Needs Checklist provided in Figure 14.1 will serve as a guide.

2. *Encourage employees to stretch their capabilities.* Continuous learning demands energy and commitment. Employees welcome the challenge to become the best they can be.

3. *Continuously question the "conventional wisdom."* Ask the "what if" questions. Questioning is possible only in an environment where it is encouraged to look at new possibilities.

4. *Support risk takers.* Make heroes out of people who come up with new ideas.

5. *Allow people to change.* Management need to understand that personal change is a psychodynamic process requiring a considerable amount of time.

6. *Create opportunities for managers and employees to receive feedback.* Managers in particular need to have information on how they are perceived by subordinates. A variety of instruments have been developed to facilitate the feedback process. People can benefit from feedback only if it is given in an environment that is supportive of personal growth and development. An increasing number of companies are recognizing the value of personal coaching as a means of developing executives and managers.

7. *Use the compensation system to reinforce expansion of employee skills portfolios.* The more that employees broaden their skills, the more value they are likely to add to the company.

8. *Create opportunities for learning new skills.* Cross-training allows a company to more quickly respond to changing needs of customers.

THE CHALLENGE: CREATING A PROCESS
OF CONTINUOUS REEDUCATION

Dan Tobin describes learning as the key to *maintaining* a high level of competitiveness. Like Tobin, I believe that in an operating environment that is undergoing fundamental change, the need for ongoing learning is critical to survival. Companies are now having to adjust to an environment where the core assumptions are changing after almost 200 years of bureaucratic top-down management. The only way to adapt and stay in front of the competition is through continuous learning.

To sum up, RapidResponse management enables the organization to move into the high-performance mode and continuous learning makes it possible to *sustain* this level of performance. Without a program for ongoing learning the organization will stagnate and lose the ability to innovate. In other words, RapidResponse management practices get the enterprise up to speed and a program of learning allows the organization to *maintain* its competitive edge.

In this chapter I have focused on how to maintain a high degree of organizational competitiveness through a program of continuous learning. The goal is to create the organization that has a high level of intelligence. To use a sports analogy, the RapidResponse organization must stay in top shape. It follows logically that the *individual employee* must also keep himself or herself in good shape. As I have explained, the RapidResponse environment demands continuous learning and continuous change. These demands can be exhausting and can lead to burnout. How to maintain balance and a sense of perspective in the face of these demands will be the subject of Chapter Fifteen.

Creating a Resilient Organization:
Lesson 14

The resilient organization has the capacity for continual adaptation to change. Continuous adaptation requires continuous learning. Tomorrow's responsive and resilient work organization will be a place in which innovation and creativity are an integral part of the culture.

CHAPTER 15

HOW TO MANAGE STRESS AND MAINTAIN HIGH ENERGY

"Is this all there is to life?" This introspective and rather agonizing question is heard with increasing frequency in the workplace. Behind the question is the frustration people are experiencing in maintaining balance between work and the other dimensions of life. People are wondering how they can keep work and career from completely dominating their lives; they are concerned about keeping their work life in proper perspective.

To stay at the cutting edge in the modern business environment requires continuous learning and growing. The secretary who learned how to work on the typewriter must develop competence with new computer technology: The same holds true for the accountant or the graphic artist. The task of developing new skills and competencies is emotionally and intellectually exhausting, and in the process of trying to stay on top, work can become an all-consuming activity. Not surprisingly, employees are now asking themselves if there is more to life than work.

The sentiment expressed recently by an associate—I'll call her Margaret—is representative of what I have heard from many women

215

over the past five years. "Career success isn't everything that we were told it would be," was the comment of this 30-something mother of two. While women like Margaret understand how their lives are enriched by multiple roles, they are also left feeling exhausted from the demands of the job and their role in the home. Increasingly, I hear both men and women say that they are working harder but the overall quality of life has not improved significantly. There is a pervasive feeling that economic conditions are insecure and that the future is uncertain.

The task of transforming an older work organization into the kind of RapidResponse enterprise described in this book demands high levels of commitment by managers and employees. Paradigm shifting will severely test the inner resources of everyone, as there is a danger that the efforts to transform the organization might cause other aspects of life to be neglected. This danger must be guarded against.

A work environment in which people are constantly stressed out and pushing themselves to the limit is not a requirement for success. The RapidResponse model presented in this book is based on the idea that there should be a balance between the personal interests of the employee and the interests of the enterprise. In sports, it is clearly understood that the players must be in good shape if the team is to win. Likewise, it is impossible to sustain high performance in any work organization if employees are angry, frustrated, tired, conflicted, or depressed. Physical and emotional well-being are prerequisites for making a creative contribution to the organization.

The ancient Romans promoted the ideal of the "four-square man." This was an individual who had developed all dimensions of his or her life through developing the physical, emotional, spiritual, and intellectual aspects of life. It is obvious that many people these days are living one-dimensional lives.

The focus of this chapter will be on the things that can be done to "stay in shape." We will look at this question from two perspectives:

1. What the *organization* can do to promote the well-being of employees

2. What *individuals* can do to maintain balance in their lives and to keep their batteries charged

STAYING FIT:
WHAT THE ORGANIZATION CAN DO

The RapidResponse model as presented in this book is a prescription for a person-centered work organization. At the heart of this model is the idea that employees are genuine insiders with a stake in the success of the enterprise. Having a stake makes people feel good about themselves and their contribution to the organization. Employees who feel invested in the enterprise are less likely to experience severe anxiety over job security because they know they are considered intelligent and mature enough to be an integral part of a winning team.

Beyond treating employees as insiders, there are other things that can be done by management to develop the inner resources of the employee. Of course it makes good business sense to encourage employees to take good care of themselves. The following list is illustrative of what management can do to promote the well-being of the individual within the organization:

1. Make it possible for people to enjoy some things about their work.

Laughter is good medicine. People who enjoy their work life are more likely to enjoy good health. For many people, the workplace is a place to have their social needs met. There is nothing wrong with this; indeed, there is a positive relationship between employees enjoying themselves, and good performance. Management should remember that there are numerous ways of creating enjoyment and goodwill at the workplace. All it takes is some creativity.

2. Drive out fear.

This was the admonition of the late Edwards Deming. Anger, hostility, and resentment bog down the workplace. I am continually amazed at the willingness of executives and managers to accept extreme conflict and low morale as a normal part of organizational life. Managers and employees should understand that intense negativity has a most detrimental effect on the health and energy levels of employees. If there is prolonged conflict, management should retain the services of a professional to address the problem.

3. Help employees keep the job in perspective.

The coaches of a professional team place a high priority on keeping the team healthy and physically fit for the entire season. This is a good model for executives and managers. It makes no sense to burn out employees to achieve short-term results. The good manager recognizes when an employee needs to recharge the batteries. Some things that management can do to sustain the energy level of employees are:

- Provide opportunities for physical exercise if the work is sedentary
- Provide psychological counseling for employees who are experiencing high levels of stress
- Create opportunities for employees to openly discuss their concerns

4. Provide positive feedback on performance.

My colleague Ken Blanchard wrote a best-selling book on the importance of making people feel good about their work. The precepts contained in *The One Minute Manager* are as relevant today as when Blanchard published his book in 1982. There is abundant research to support the idea that recognition, achievement, and the ability to share responsibility are the best motivators of employees. Employees who feel psychologically fulfilled are more likely to feel energized and fit.

5. Encourage employees to work smarter, not harder.

In Chapter Five we described a methodology that can be used to simplify work processes. It is obvious that much of the frustration experienced by employees is built into the work process. In every work organization, there are opportunities for making work easier and simpler.

The culture in some companies places a priority on spending long hours in the office. There is the mistaken assumption that the employee who spends extra hours at work will be more productive. In fact, creativity and productivity tend to diminish after a certain amount of time.

6. Manage the stress level within the organization.

Management need to continually monitor the stress level within the organization. Usually the symptoms of stress are very obvious—drug abuse, increased absenteeism, and intergroup conflict. Sometimes the stress is a result of poor communication. Organizational stressors include the physical work space, unhealthy competition, and conflicting values. A major priority for management is the removal of unnecessary stressors whenever possible.

STAYING FIT: WHAT YOU CAN DO FOR YOURSELF

The responsibility for maintaining a sense of balance in one's life cannot be delegated to any organization. Enlightened organizations that are interested in the long term will promote the practices just outlined; however, in today's work environment, individuals must assume the primary responsibility for keeping themselves in good shape. A whole book could be written on the things that the individual can do to promote their own emotional, intellectual, and physical development. The following list is indicative of the kinds of things that each person can do to promote good health and well-being.

1. Maintain balance in your life.

The Life-style Grid, illustrated in Figure 15.1, shows the four key dimensions of each person's life. The grid, as shown, represents a perfectly balanced life with time devoted to the job, the home, social

Career	Home
Social	Self

Figure 15.1.
The Life-style Grid: "the balanced life."

life, and personal development. This is the ideal. The Life-style Grid
suggests a balance among four priorities:

Work. This is the time spent earning a living.

Home. This is time spent with family. This may be a nuclear
family, an extended family of friends, or a significant other.

Social. This is the time spent interacting with people outside the
home or the workplace. Introverted people need to pay particular attention to this dimension of their life.

Self. This is the time we have for ourselves. It allows us to
recharge our batteries. Extroverted people need to pay particular
attention to this dimension of their life.

Figure 15.2 illustrates the *imbalance* that can be found in the
lives of so many individuals at this time. There is a tendency for people at different stages in their career to have different priorities.
Earlier we discussed the struggle that career women have in maintaining a balance between workplace responsibilities and the
demands of the home. Both men and women can have difficulty nur-

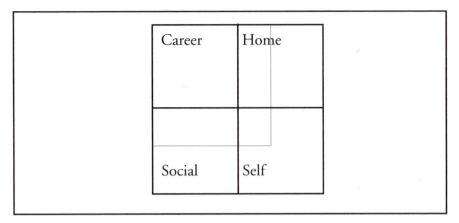

Figure 15.2.
Life-style Grid: "the career-dominated life."

turing social relationships outside of work because of the demands of the job.

The Life-style Grid emphasizes the need to work toward living a balanced life recognizing that priorities will change over time. It is a reminder that there is more to life than work and career.

2. Stay focused.

People need to have a sense of purpose if they are to maintain balance in their lives. Individuals have different opinions about making money; my view is that money is not the purpose of life but a *requirement* for accomplishing more worthy goals. Whatever your beliefs, the important issue is that we have a sense of direction and purpose in our lives. Some things that people can do to help stay focused and centered include

- Spending time meditating or reflecting
- Practicing yoga
- Going on a retreat
- Scheduling solitary time such as a walk on the beach

3. Stay physically fit.

Just about everyone now understands that there is a very close correlation between regular exercise and emotional well-being. Membership in a fitness center may be the best insurance you can have. One of the paradoxes of life is that we have increased energy when we engage in increased physical activity.

4. Be able to articulate your own core values.

These values may be rooted in religious belief or upbringing. It is easier to cope with the setbacks in life when one's life is anchored in transcendent values.

5. Enjoy time at work and time away from work.

Some people think of work as the punishment they endure so that they are in a position to enjoy the rest of their lives. This mentality has a very limiting effect on the enjoyment of life since we spend so many hours in the workplace. Our attitude toward work should be reevaluated on a regular basis.

6. Don't overidentify with the job.

Your job should not define who you are. John Lucas, the NBA basketball coach, reminds players that basketball is a game that they play, not who they are. He wants his players to leave the game and know that there are many other things they can do with their lives.

7. Manage time.

How do we *manage* ourselves? We can't make more time, but we can manage to make good use of the time that we have. Sometimes the simplest self-management techniques, such as the daily "to do" list, are most effective.

8. Change negative self-defeating messages.

Negative messages have a way of becoming self-fulfilling prophecies. It is easy to get depressed about a lot of things. However, the simple truth is that those who maintain a positive attitude are more resourceful in dealing with the ups and downs of life.

9. Know your limitations.

In today's fast-changing environment, there is a danger of burning the candle at both ends. One reason to have good friends is that they remind us when it is time to slow down.

Love Your Job

My colleague Dr. Paul Powers argues that people should learn to enjoy their work or else find a job that they like. In a thought-provoking book, *Love Your Job* (Sebastopol, CA.: O'Reilly & Associates, 1993), Powers and his collaborator, Deborah Russell, provide practical insights on ways of gaining psychological satisfaction in the workplace. Here are five suggestions from *Love Your Job*:

1. *Dream a big dream.* Most of us have dreams and jobs too small for our spirits. Let your mind and heart take flight. What would you truly love to do?

2. *Don't settle for too little.* Your time at work isn't a dress rehearsal for something better. During your lifetime you'll spend about 100,000 hours—nearly half the waking hours of your adult life—at work. Don't waste any of those hours.

3. *Play the hand that's dealt you.* There are ups and downs in every job. Its how we handle those ups and downs that makes the difference.

4. *Challenge yourself.* A job isn't static, and neither are you. Even the most satisfying job won't remain so if it doesn't grow along with you and challenge you to keep growing, too.

5. *Recharge your batteries.* People who love their jobs the most aren't necessarily workaholics. Reserve time and emotional energy for all the other important parts of your life.

KEEP FIRST THINGS FIRST

This chapter can be summed up in one expression: *Keep first things first.* The challenge is to maintain a sense of perspective and not to lose sight of what is really important. Income from the job can ideally be seen as making it possible to meet responsibilities to self, family, and society. However, the job should not totally consume our lives. As I have indicated, it is easy to get caught on the fast-moving treadmill, burn out the batteries, and lose sight of the noncareer aspects of one's life.

To be successful in today's stressful environment requires having a clear set of values and the ability to maintain a balance between personal and career priorities. Because some of society's traditional anchors have disappeared, it can be difficult staying centered and maintaining focus. This makes it all the more important to be able to go within ourselves to draw strength and inspiration.

If we want to contribute to the organization, we have to continually nurture and develop our own spiritual, emotional, physical, and intellectual resources. A person who is constantly "giving" runs the risk of coming up empty. In my work as an advisor to management, I have learned of the importance of replenishing myself. Some of this inner renewal comes from going within and taking time to process what I am doing. A network of friends and associates is also a source of strength and replenishment. Each person needs to develop their own customized program of self-care. A tough job demands a healthy life-style. Those that are fit will be in a position to make the most creative contribution.

Creating the Resilient Organization:
Lesson 15

The overall strategy for building the resilient organization must include attention to maintaining and increasing the energy level of employees. When workers wear down and start suffering from "battle fatigue," they have a tendency toward cynicism and negativity.

C H A P T E R   1 6

WIDER APPLICATIONS OF RAPIDRESPONSE MANAGEMENT:
Education, Professional Services, Government Agencies

Throughout this book I have used mature business and industrial organizations to illustrate the possibilities offered by the RapidResponse approach. This choice is not surprising as RapidResponse was born out of DGI's work with business and industry. However, we have also been able to apply these precepts successfully to other kinds of work environments.

It is not just mature businesses that face the change-or-perish challenge. In this chapter I explore the possibilities for applying RapidResponse to education, public, and professional services.

Several years ago, as I was listening one evening to NPR's "Marketplace" on my car radio, a casual comment caught my attention. James Autry, the poet-laureate of the business community, was talking about how different organizations respond to change. Autry asserted that *businesses* were more capable of making changes than nonbusiness organizations such as schools or other not-for-profit organizations. As I reflected on his comments I realized that what James Autry was saying made a lot of sense. For business, making changes is a matter of survival. The economic realities enter into the picture. The pressures of the marketplace are not felt with the same intensity or immediacy by your local high school or by the state Department of Highways. In the past not-for-profit organizations have been somewhat insulated from the forces of the marketplace.

This chapter takes the RapidResponse concept and applies it to three important areas of activity. The basic premise is that the old paradigm of service delivery is no longer satisfactory; the people who "pay the freight," the customers, are demanding a higher level of responsiveness to their needs. The pressures of the marketplace are now being felt by organizations and institutions that previously operated with a considerable degree of detachment.

The discussion of how RapidResponse can be applied beyond the business and industry will focus on three areas of service activity:

- Education/ schools and colleges
- Governmental services
- Professional services

APPLYING RAPIDRESPONSE TO EDUCATION

Since the late 1970s I have had the opportunity to consult with over 50 school systems in the United States and in the Republic of Ireland. This work has primarily involved team-building workshops for classroom teachers and leadership training for administrators. What I have observed through all these experiences, particularly in the public schools, is somewhat depressing.

In a normal classroom teachers "dish out" out information while students listen passively. This method of teaching has led to extreme dissatisfaction: Numerous teachers, especially those in their middle years, speak of having lost the interest and the energy to engage their students. In every team-building workshop, dysfunctional behavior was evident, including strong hostility and passive-aggressive behavior. Indeed, the adversarial relationship between management and teacher was often more intense than the labor-management relationship observed in business and industrial organizations.

Teachers frequently viewed parents and school committee members in adversarial terms; the concept of parent or student as "customer" was nonexistent; high levels of cynicism and burnout were present in almost every teacher and administrator group. Ironically, there was little difference between what I observed in schools in the United States and in the Republic of Ireland. Most noticeable in management development sessions for administrators was an absence of vision. Among teachers humor and laughter were most notably absent. Sometimes the feelings of tension could be picked up by simply walking into the faculty room during lunch hour.

"I GET NO RESPECT!"

Many teachers spoke of feeling undervalued by administrators, parents, students, and the community. Rarely did I encounter teachers who saw school committee members as their supporters or advocates. The words "learned helplessness" aptly describe the lack of empowerment experienced by teachers in first- and second-level schools.

Low self-esteem among faculty is not the only problem I observed. In my view, the level of resistance to change among teachers is stronger than that typically found in business organizations. Teachers do not generally like any disruption in the status quo: "We always did it this way" is frequently heard. The following anecdote will serve to illustrate.

Joan, a first grade teacher, decided to pursue a graduate degree in education at a local university. She became a strong believer in interactive education and began to introduce the new ideas in her classroom. Other teachers from the second and third grades immediately protested to the principal, fearing that Joan's efforts would create different expectations on the part of the children. After over 20 years in the classroom these teachers were not inclined to change the way they performed.

SCHOOLS NEED RADICAL TRANSFORMATION

The reader may consider these comments to be a harsh indictment of teachers or school administrators. They are not intended as such—

schools often have no incentive to change. Rather, I hope to make clear that the school, *as a work environment,* needs to undergo a radical transformation. There is no need to scapegoat the teachers or the administrators. It should also be pointed out that the winds of change can be found in some school districts. The movement toward school-based management is gathering momentum. Innovative schools are emerging around the country.

The three core tenets of the RapidResponse environment provide a basis for radically transforming the school from an anemic soul-destroying institution into a place that is percolating with positive energy. The process of transforming the school is not different from that of transforming a community hospital or an old manufacturing company. It begins with business education. The more closely teachers can identify with those who pay their salary, the people who pay taxes, the more likely they are to be responsive; with the growth of school system bureaucracies, teachers have become too removed from their "customers."

Teachers are *not* given the respect by administrators that they deserve. These administrators often lack the management skills needed to empower teachers, to make them feel they are active participants in the process of redesigning the classroom experience. Administrators practice a patriarchal style of management that they first cultivated in the classroom. When school bureaucrats treat teachers in an infantile manner, they are destroying the self-esteem and professionalism of the teacher. At a time when the classroom requires dynamic interactive learning, teachers often resign themselves to a passive information-sharing approach.

The time has come to give teachers incentives for producing good results. I know that some will consider it sacrilegious to speak of tying classroom performance to financial gain; given the traditional "public service paradigm," there is a reluctance to introduce evaluation criteria or to tie performance to monetary rewards. But marketplace forces necessitate radical changes in schools. The token in-service training now being offered to teachers and administrators is certainly not the answer to the problem.

THE CHALLENGES CONFRONTING COLLEGES

While colleges and universities are more responsive to the marketplace than first- and second-level schools, these institutions can benefit from the application of RapidResponse precepts. In the future, small liberal arts colleges with declining enrollment will need to move quickly into new markets. Teaching faculty, with their detached attitudes, will need to become more involved in promoting the services of the institution. For these faculty, becoming market focused will require a paradigm shift. Administrators and faculty will need to understand that their job security is dependent on the ability to meet the changing needs of stakeholders. A "take it or leave it" attitude is a recipe for failure.

Colleges and universities are notorious for unfriendly processes: Students are often confronted with an oppressive and unwieldy bureaucracy when they want to carry out even the smallest transaction. As the marketplace for students becomes increasingly competitive, institutions will need to develop more efficient user-friendly business processes. Adapting to change is not part of the culture of academic institutions, and it will probably take pressure from the marketplace to bring about any kind of meaningful streamlining of systems and processes in colleges and universities. These institutions will eventually have to undergo the kind of process redesign that was outlined in Chapter Five.

This discussion of the application of RapidResponse precepts to the field of education can be summarized as follows:

- The future of society is dependent on schools that inspire students to learn and grow. To accomplish this goal, schools will need to become less bureaucratic and more customer centered.

- Schools need to be redesigned in such a way as to make teachers feel they have a real investment in the overall performance of the school.

- The application of RapidResponse precepts provides the basis for transforming schools into high-performance organizations.

APPLICATION OF RAPIDRESPONSE
TO THE PUBLIC SECTOR

There is growing discontent among taxpayers over the level of service provided by public agencies. Political candidates who engage in government bashing strike a responsive chord; introduce the subject of government services and someone will come up with a horror story. Despite all the talk about "reinventing government," however, unwieldy bureaucracy remains endemic in agencies and institutions providing government services.

Though we tend to blame the individuals who work in public organizations, blaming the civil servant for poor service is analogous to blaming the teacher for the low quality of education. In each case, the *work environment* operates on a set of assumptions that frustrate and destroy even the most committed members of staff. The following case study illustrates the root causes of the poor service provided by public agencies.

THE DINOSAUR COURTHOUSE

In 1992 I was invited by the administrator of a county courthouse to give input on how total quality management (TQM) could be introduced. This project was part of a statewide effort to introduce TQM as a means of improving services to the public. As the administrator described the courthouse operation, I began to wonder how this institution could possibly respond to any "customers." Within the courthouse were employees who were answerable to the district judge, the county sheriff, the county commissioners, and several state agencies. Each group operated as an autonomous entity—often in open competition with another group. The work processes within the courthouse could have been designed by a madman! Redundant time-consuming activities were built into almost every work process. It would have been impossible under the existing conditions to give good service to the public. There were numerous examples of dysfunctional behavior on the part of courthouse employees. It was evident from just walking around the courthouse that employees were angry, frustrated, and experiencing low morale. Conflict had become accepted as an integral part of the organization's culture.

My conclusion, after two discussions with the administrator, was that I did not want to be associated with efforts to introduce TQM. The idea of getting together some groups of unempowered employees to do incremental improvements of microprocesses had no appeal to me; it would be tantamount to applying a small Band Aid where major surgery was needed. I know that to turn the courthouse into an enterprise capable of providing fast user-friendly services would require a complete transformation of organizational culture. Core processes would need to be radically redesigned from end to end. As a first step the key stakeholders would need to come together to formulate a vision of what the courthouse could become. There would need to be an acknowledgment that this organization, with its antiquated work practices, had outlived its ability to meet the expectations of its "customers."

It takes courageous leadership to bring about the kind of changes that are needed in agencies or institutions that have the mind-set of the county courthouse. Employees become stuck in a bureaucratic way of thinking. The change strategies described in Chapters Ten and Eleven can all be used to help bring about the cultural transformation. The courthouse and similarly bureaucratic government service agencies are fertile ground for the precepts of RapidResponse management. Among the growing number of national leaders advocating the "reinventing" of government agencies are Al Gore, Newt Gingrich, Ross Perot, and Robert Reich. Governors are also leading the way.

As I have already explained, token incremental solutions will not create the kind of dynamic work environment needed for responsive delivery of services. Installing some desktop computers will do nothing more than create the illusion of solving the problem; new information technology must to be part of a culture change. Old work practices need to be put under the microscope and redesigned to better serve those who use services. The degree of difficulty involved in bringing about a radical cultural transformation cannot be overstated: People who work in public agencies have had years of socialization in bureaucratic ways of thinking.

GOVERNMENT CAN SERVE THE PEOPLE

The courthouse story serves to illustrate an important point: *Government bureaucracies are not designed to be highly responsive to their "customers."* However, the consumer of government services tends to personalize the problem and to scapegoat the civil servant. The typical reaction is not to say "This is a dinosaur organization," but to say "These people have a bad attitude." What is seldom understood is that these bureaucracies destroy much of what is good and noble in the people who work within them. Dysfunctional organizations tend to create dysfunctional people.

What if civil servants were imbued with the entrepreneurial spirit and citizens were treated as real customers? The following case study suggests that the RapidResponse government agency could be a pleasant place to visit.

Over the years I have considered a trip to the Registry of Motor Vehicles to be in the same category as a trip to the dentist office: a less than pleasant experience to say the least. You feel like you are part of a herd of cattle; employees seem unhappy and uptight; get in the wrong line, and you're delayed for an additional 45 minutes. The trip to the Registry does nothing to enhance self-esteem.

My view underwent a radical change over the past six months. While shopping at the local mall, I had noticed a new walk-in office of the Registry of Motor Vehicles. A visit to this office several weeks later provided some pleasant surprises. The warm greeting and the invitation to have a seat seemed out of place for a government agency! Within a few minutes my license photo was taken and the employee said that I could either go and have a cup a coffee and pick it up later or wait until the license was laminated. I walked out with my new license after a 10-minute visit that left me feeling that I was an important *customer*.

The drivers licence office in the mall illustrates the fact that federal, state, and local agencies do not have to be insensitive bureaucracies. The possibilities for radical improvements are numerous. In some instances, change may mean redesigning physical space as in the case of the Registry; in almost every situation, information technology can be used to enhance the delivery of services. Public agencies are only beginning to discover the power of the computer to enhance

Endless Possibilities

The Registrar of Motor Vehicles in Massachusetts, Jerold Gnazzo, is quick to point out that he was recruited by Governor William Weld because of his business background. Gnazzo's entrepreneurial orientation comes across as he talks about making it easy for his "customers" to access services. The agency he inherited had a well-deserved reputation for unfriendly bureaucratic service delivery.

It is clear that what Gnazzo has in mind is a RapidResponse Registry of Motor Vehicles. He talks about the "endless possibilities" for creating easy access to Registry services. Some of the innovations already introduced or in the process of implementation include

- *License Express:* bringing license renewal services to convenient mall locations. These offices are modeled on the customer service centers that can be found in the business community.
- *Credit Card Payment:* expediting citation and fee payment by phone or by mail. A citizen can renew car registration by making a phone call and giving his or her credit card number.
- *Automated License Scheduling and Testing:* eliminating 40 years of taxpayers' time spent waiting in line. Formerly, the citizen who was getting a new license had to make a special trip to the Registry office just to schedule the road test. Now the test can be scheduled by a phone call.
- *One-Stop Commercial Vehicle Center:* combining six agencies under one roof. In the past, a trucker would have to negotiate through six separate state or county agencies to complete the paperwork. A new experimental center makes it possible to do everything at one location.
- *Drive:* allowing remote registration through dealers. One of the unpleasant tasks associated with buying a new car in the past was the time-consuming trip to the Registry of Motor Vehicles. That step will be eliminated.

One of the more subtle changes has been attitudinal. Gnazzo is frequently asked what he has done to change the attitudes of his state employees. His response: "I haven't worked on attitudes, *I've worked on changing the environment in which services are delivered.*"

their efforts to serve the public. One of the best examples is the local library; instant access to databases is now available at most locations.

To sum up, we can say that

- Most public agencies are capable of been transformed into efficient, customer-driven entities.
- The foundation for building the RapidResponse public agency is a process of reeducation that creates a heightened awareness of the needs of "customers."
- The transformation of public agencies involves both the streamlining of core work processes and a transformation in the mind-set of employees.

APPLICATION OF RAPIDRESPONSE TO PROFESSIONAL SERVICES DELIVERY

In the case of schools and public service agencies, growing pressures to be more responsive are coming from citizens who want a return for their taxes. The level of expectation on the part of citizens will continue to rise. There is, in addition, one other group that is facing increased pressure to make changes, and that is the provider of professional services. In this case, the pressure is coming from the marketplace. Traditionally, many professionals have been able to maintain a somewhat detached attitude. Like public servants and educators, these professionals would not have considered responsiveness to their "customer" to be a high priority. Now, pressure from consumers is causing the need for a paradigm shift.

The following three examples illustrate the dilemma confronting professional service providers.

Example 1.

In 1991, one of my colleagues and I conducted a one-day workshop for psychologists on "Marketing Professional Services." It was clear that participants were fearful of the changes taking place as a result of managed care and other market-driven developments. All these psychologists had been told during their training that it was unethical for them to try to "sell" their services. At one time during the workshop, a young Ph.D. declared that he "would die before he became a marketer of himself and his services." It was obvious that this statement struck a responsive chord with others in the group. Similar sentiments are frequently expressed by physicians who see their security threatened by the advent of managed care but who are extremely reluctant to make changes.

Example 2.

In the early 1990s I spoke to a statewide CPA organization on "Doing Business in the New Business Environment." In preparation for the presentation I interviewed five accountants. What was noteworthy was the degree of fear and anger expressed by each individual over the way change was affecting their professional practice. All expressed concern that the growing popularity of accounting software would make their skills obsolete.

Example 3.

In the recent past, I heard an individual talk about the changes that were affecting his work as a professional speaker. He complained that meeting planners and speaking bureaus were now expecting him to accept assignments on as little as a month's notice, whereas in the past he could plan his schedule six months in advance.

Each of these examples points in a common direction: *Those who provide professional services are having to make a paradigm shift in the way they deliver services.* It is clear in each case that quickness in becoming responsive to the changes in the marketplace will be the key to survival and success. While professionals typically do not have to deal with a large unwieldy bureaucracy, they do need to develop a new mind-set. They must learn to "listen" to what the market is telling them.

To sum up, a new paradigm is emerging for professional service delivery. It will require professionals and professional services firms to be more responsive to the marketplace. The winners will be those who are capable of a quick and effective response.

THE FORMULA FOR SUCCESS:
CUSTOMER RESPONSIVENESS

In this chapter we have explored how RapidResponse precepts can be applied in such sectors as education, public service agencies, and the delivery of professional services. Like business and industry, these sectors are having to adjust to changing expectations. They must learn how to become more responsive to those who use their services. They need to create a more market-focused mind-set among employees.

Two examples will serve to illustrate the level of responsiveness needed for success in tomorrow's marketplace. While these examples come from the retail services sector, they have universal application.

Recently a colleague told me about an interesting experience he had in a fast-food restaurant. As he looked over the menu he was attracted to the colorful flask that was offered at a discounted price. The flask came filled with a well-known beverage. My colleague wanted to buy the flask but with a different beverage. Knowing that most fast-food workers are trained to act in a robotlike manner, he hesitated before asking the 15-year-old if he could buy the flask at sale price with a different beverage. "Mister, this is America! You can have anything you want!" was the response. This young person had an intuitive understanding of what it takes to be successful in the new business environment.

The second example comes from a recent personal experience. As I was writing the manuscript for this book, the laser-jet printer developed problems. In making the call to the Hewlett-Packard customer service office I expected questions about the warranty, the date of purchase, and how the equipment had been used. What a pleasant surprise! The woman who took the call expressed regret over any inconvenience, told me that she would have FedEx pick up the printer the next morning, and indicated that the turn-around time would be less than one week. I was made to feel like a valued *customer*.

The assumptions underlying these experiences can be applied by your local physician, the school in your neighborhood, or at City Hall. The fast-food worker and the H-P representative both understood the importance of responding to the needs of the marketplace.

For some individuals and organizations the change will require a 360-degree transformation in the way business is transacted. The recipe for developing the *responsive* services organization is the same as for other sectors of the business community: Streamline delivery processes and instill the entrepreneurial spirit in employees.

RapidResponse precepts are as relevant to the delivery of public and professional services as to business and industry. The need to be nimble and responsive is not confined to any particular sector of the economy. The Age of Bureaucracy is over. RapidResponse is the new paradigm for service delivery.

Creating the Resilient Organization: Lesson 16

The basic principles of RapidResponse management have applications beyond business and industry in educational, professional, and governmental agencies and institutions. All these organizations are confronted with the need for increased responsiveness and resiliency. The biggest challenge is to create work environments that capitalize on the natural *entrepreneurial* instincts of employees. The need to be market-focused applies to all sectors of the economy.

CHAPTER 17

UNLEASHING THE ENTREPRENEURIAL SPIRIT

Pick up any current business journal and you will find an article detailing the evils of bureaucratic management. There is a growing recognition that bureaucracy is a deadly disease that pervades the modern workplace. However, almost every company exhibits bureaucratic tendencies. These companies shun the risk taker and reward those with expertise in playing the bureaucratic game. They favor top-down decision making. The bureaucratic culture leads inevitably to missed opportunities in the marketplace.

Business leaders have become aware of the need to prune bureaucratic practices out of older organizations. Unfortunately, these leaders tend to look for solutions in the wrong places or to adapt changes that fall far short of the mark. The list of "cures" in recent years has included everything from total quality management to business process reengineering to just-in-time inventory management. Some companies have chopped management layers and decentralized. All these partial remedies, though useful, fail to unleash the entrepreneurial spirit. The challenge confronting management is to find a way to put the spirit of enterprise back into organizations that are suffering from the bureaucratic disease.

THE ENTREPRENEURIAL ORGANIZATION: FOUR CHARACTERISTICS

In this book we have described the revitalized work organization as a RapidResponse enterprise. It is an organization in which workers and managers see themselves as part of an entrepreneurial endeavor. The characteristics of the truly entrepreneurial company are easily recognizable. We can summarize this discussion of RapidResponse management by briefly identifying four key characteristics of the entrepreneurial enterprise:

1. Entrepreneurial companies are opportunistic.

Successful entrepreneurial companies find and exploit markets that others have missed. The opportunism comes from the fact that they are "wired in" to the marketplace. However, these companies do not merely identify the market opportunity, but they are able to act quickly enough to capitalize on the situation.

The culture of many large bureaucratic companies is destructive of the entrepreneurial spirit. These "elephants" become blind to the opportunities that surround them. They tend to punish, rather than reward, risk taking. When a company shoots the champions, everyone gets the message.

2. Entrepreneurial companies have employees who act as owners.

Entrepreneurs are owners. In the entrepreneurial company employees have an owner mentality. They feel as if they are treated as owners who can keep the rewards if they are successful but who also suffer the consequences if not. Their personal investment in the success of the enterprise provides a unique motivation, both economic and psychological.

The larger the company, the more difficult it is to promote the owner mentality. It is impossible to create this sense of ownership without the generous sharing of business information with people at every level. However, the sharing must go beyond business literacy to the actual sharing in after-tax profits. Incentive compensation systems have the effect of creating an entrepreneurial mentality.

Traditional bureaucratic companies have compensation structures that discourage entrepreneurial activity. In these companies the pay scale is often based on factors that have nothing to do with entrepreneurial endeavor. Endurance in the job becomes a guarantee of automatic increases in compensation. People come to view their compensation as an entitlement that has little relationship to the value that they add to the enterprise.

In the truly entrepreneurial company the pay system is designed to help both managers and rank-and-file employees think like owners. Compensation is tied to the value that the individual brings to the enterprise. A new objective measure called economic value added (EVA) is now used in progressive companies in determining the incentives that will be shared with managers and workers. EVA calculates the true economic profit on earnings after subtracting the cost of capital.

3. Entrepreneurial companies are nimble and agile.

Unlike their bureaucratic counterparts, entrepreneurial companies have the flexibility and agility to respond quickly to changing conditions in the marketplace. One of the reasons for this responsiveness is the fact that lower-level people are encouraged to think and act on their own.

Many companies are too hierarchical and bureaucratic. In some of these companies an ordinary business transaction can require as many as 20 signatures. In the entrepreneurial environment people are focused on responding to the customer rather than on bureaucratic procedures.

The first step in creating an entrepreneurial orientation is to reduce or eliminate the hierarchy. However, removing layers of white-collar workers will not necessarily produce the speed and agility that is needed in today's marketplace. The more difficult challenge is to change behavior patterns. Decision-making should be pushed downward, and corporate oversight kept to the minimum. Cumbersome bureaucratic work processes must be redesigned to create a free flow of activity in the direction of the marketplace. Without some form of organizational surgery bureaucratic organizations will not have the ability to make the quick navigational adjustments required in today's and tomorrow's marketplace.

4. Entrepreneurial organizations have a team culture.

One of the characteristics of a truly entrepreneurial enterprise is that everyone acts as if he or she was a *team* player. People are concerned about the company as well as about themselves. A strong sense of common purpose can be found throughout the organization. This may or may not include the use of formal teams to accomplish company goals. In contrast, the culture of large bureaucratic companies discourages teamwork. Individualism is rewarded. In the bureaucratic environment people are not judged by their effort or by the value they create. The emphasis is on status and the trappings of power and influence.

In successful entrepreneurial companies status follows performance. The rewards of success are value adding, such as stock options. Every individual is made to feel that he or she is a key player on the team. Winning in the marketplace is considered more important than individual success.

In the truly entrepreneurial enterprise, morale problems are nonexistent. The thrill of winning is shared by everyone. People want to contribute to the maximum. The workplace becomes a learning laboratory where each person can continuously improve his or her skills.

SEVEN STEPS TO BEING RESPONSIVE

In tomorrow's highly dynamic business environment, the leader will need to be like a fighter pilot who continuously responds to new and unexpected treats in the environment. The ability to quickly correct mistakes or miscalculations will be a key survival skill. Here are some steps that the leader can take to create and maintain an organization that is responsive to changes in the environment.

1. *Communicate with employees as if survival depended on it.* The goal: Get people focused on external reality—customers and competitors.

2. *Make entrepreneurs out of employees.* In the modern business environment the enduring advantages will be with companies who make better use of people. However, real commitment can only come in a work environment where employees believe they have a vested interest in the success of the corporation.

3. *Use process mapping.* Break the organization down into a few core processes. Map out these processes, identify the inefficiencies and then redesign each process to serve the customer in the most efficient manner possible.

4. *Continuously reeducate the organization.* Transforming any business is not an event but an enduring process that needs to be sustained. Knowledge is the lubrication that keeps the organization in a state of readiness for new developments in the marketplace.

5. *Let everyone see the opportunities as well as the dangers involved in change.* The message to employees: It is the nimble that will survive and prosper.

6. *Keep in mind that all change is personal.* As I have previously noted, the late Thomas "Tip" O'Neill was fond of saying that "all politics are local." It is equally true that all change ultimately involves *individuals.* The human side of change must not be neglected.

7. *Pay attention to the human dimension.* During a period of change people will become very stressed out. Promote activities that support the emotional and physical well-being of employees. The lesson from the sports world: Only those who are in good shape have what it takes to win.

A RACE AGAINST TIME

It is estimated that only 5% of all U.S. businesses operate according to the high-performance principles presented in this book. This leads to a question: Why is it that so many companies continue to cling to the old bureaucratic practices? The answer is that business leaders have not recognized the need for a *radical change* in the assumptions and behavioral patterns that exist in work organizations. Up to this time there was the belief the bureaucratic disease could be "cured" by less radical approaches.

The need to transform old bureaucracies becomes more obvious with each passing day. The major breakthrough in recent years is the recognition that the transformation process can be greatly accelerated. The blitz change strategy, developed by our consulting group, offers management a framework for converting from the bureaucratic mode to the new high-performance RapidResponse mode. For many traditional work organizations, it is a race against time. There is not the luxury of waiting several years before introducing the new high-performance concepts.

The effectiveness of any intervention will ultimately depend on the ability of the leadership to persuade people to let go of outdated management practices and to embrace the new concepts. The indispensable requirement is that the leader have a vision for the future that is both attractive and achievable. The old cliché about "teaching an old dog new tricks" is applicable when it comes to changing older established work organizations. Machiavelli recognized the problem 500 years ago. There is no easy fix.

Creating the Resilient Organization: Lesson 17

There is one overriding challenge confronting business leaders today: how to increase organizational resilience by tapping into the innate entrepreneurial aspirations of employees. The principles of RapidResponse management promote responsiveness and resiliency by unleashing the spirit of enterprise throughout the organization.

E P I L O G U E

DECLINE
OR REVITALIZATION?

The truth is finally sinking in: America is losing its global competitiveness. The warnings articulated by Richard Goodwin in *Promises to Keep* are being voiced by a growing number of political leaders, including Ross Perot. In plain Texas language, Perot has pointed to the need to "look under the hood" and to identify the underlying weaknesses. Clearly, the feelings of invincibility that were widespread just a few years ago have been replaced with fear and foreboding. Others, including Al Gore and Newt Gingrich, have joined Perot in calling for a transformation of our economic infrastructure.

The difficult challenges confronting businesses can be viewed as threats or as opportunities. I believe the leadership of our work organizations will see challenge as opportunity. There really is no middle ground: The choice is between decline and revitalization.

Because responsiveness and flexibility will determine the winners and losers in the future, the challenge is to transform bureaucratic business entities into dynamic entrepreneurial enterprises. This book presents a new vision of what the work organization can become. It provides a path to begin the process of revitalization in offices, factories, hospitals, banks, and other places of business.

Revitalization of the economy depends upon thousands of small and mid-sized companies that constitute 98% of America's economic infrastructure.

In this book we have addressed three questions:

- Why do organizations need to make fundamental changes?
- What are the essential changes that must be made?
- How can these changes be implemented?

In contemplating the answers I have offered, I hope my readers will remember:

1. An historic paradigm shift is taking place in the way businesses are managed. Alvin Toffler describes the shift as the move from the Industrial Age to the Information Age.

2. In the new business environment, speed/responsiveness will be the competitive factor.

3. A high level of employee commitment and freedom from bureaucratic constraints are the foundations on which to build a "rapid response" enterprise.

4. Transforming a traditional work organization into a high-performance enterprise requires a cultural transformation.

5. The challenge of bringing about the shift from traditional management will require leadership that has a high level of credibility with the work force.

While the problems facing older established companies are certainly not unique to the United States, Americans can lead the way in coming up with solutions. American history suggests that there is reason for optimism in facing the tough challenges of the future. The history of the United States shows constant change, even revolutionary change, to meet the needs of succeeding generations; Americans have an openness and a willingness to innovate not found in older societies. Traditionally, the greatest strength of the American manager is the "let's do it" attitude. This can-do attitude will provide the impetus for timely conversion of older companies and institutions to the RapidResponse mode of management.

While almost every company or institution has the capability to implement RapidResponse management, smaller companies are in a position to lead the way in making the difficult changes. Using the concrete suggestions given, managers should develop a plan to suit their own companies. In this way they will not merely succeed in beating the competition, but will also be helping to unleash the enormous creativity and vitality of the American people.

THE FIRST STEP:
ORGANIZATIONAL ANALYSIS

The first step in creating a resilient organization is to review existing management practices. To get a picture of your organization, have five or six employees from different levels complete the questionnaire on the following pages. The checklist contains 35 statements that characterize the high-performing RapidResponse enterprise. To score how well your organization is doing, total the points you have circled within each category. The six categories include the three core RapidResponse management practices and three factors critical to the implementation of these practices. There are a possible 25 points for each category.

RAPIDRESPONSE READINESS CHECKLIST

Section 1: Employees Have Access to the Scoreboard

	Disagree			Agree	
1. All employees understand the big picture—how the company is performing in the marketplace.	1	2	3	4	5
2. Employees have a good understanding of the wants/ needs of customers.	1	2	3	4	5
3. All employees know who the competitors are and their strengths and weaknesses.	1	2	3	4	5
4. Information is freely shared by management with employees.	1	2	3	4	5
5. Strategic objectives are effectively communicated with the entire work force.	1	2	3	4	5

Total Points =

Section 2: Work Activity Flows Freely in the Direction of the Customer

	Disagree			Agree	
1. Our company had the flexibility to adapt to new business opportunities.	1	2	3	4	5
2. The customer is clearly the focus of all activity.	1	2	3	4	5
3. Our organizational structures allow us to get the product/service to the customer in a timely manner.	1	2	3	4	5
4. The core work processes are free of needless delays, rework and nonvalue-adding activity.	1	2	3	4	5
5. In our company technology is used to increase speed to market.	1	2	3	4	5

Total points =

248

Section 3: Employees Have a Stake in the Outcome

	Disagree			Agree	
1. Employees are treated as "insiders" and given up-to-date information on the financial performance of the company.	1	2	3	4	5
2. Our compensation system makes it possible for employees to influence the amount of compensation that they receive.	1	2	3	4	5
3. Employees think of themselves as entrepreneurs with an ownership stake in the company.	1	2	3	4	5
4. The compensation system reinforces teamwork and encourages multiskill development.	1	2	3	4	5
5. Each employee can see how his/her work contributes to the success of the company.	1	2	3	4	5

Total points =

Section 4: The Business Is Positioned for Success

	Disagree			Agree	
1. Top management has a clear sense of the direction in which they are leading the company.	1	2	3	4	5
2. The vision for the future of the company is clearly communicated to all employees.	1	2	3	4	5
3. We are united in pursuit of a common goal.	1	2	3	4	5
4. Employees are more focused on the future than the "good old days."	1	2	3	4	5
5. Employees clearly understand how the business is positioned for success in the marketplace.	1	2	3	4	5

Total points =

Section 5: The Company Has Managers Who Can Lead

	Disagree			Agree	
1. We feel challenged to live up to our potential by the leaders of the company.	1	2	3	4	5
2. Top management provides visionary leadership—they know what they want the organization to become.	1	2	3	4	5
3. Employees throughout the company believe that top management is genuinely concerned about them.	1	2	3	4	5
4. There is a high level of trust and confidence in company management.	1	2	3	4	5
5. Our leaders are pioneers who are willing to accept the challenges of a fast-changing business environment.	1	2	3	4	5

Total points =

Section 6: Middle Management Is "in on the Deal"

	Disagree			Agree	
1. Middle management does not feel threatened by efforts to increase involvement by line staff.	1	2	3	4	5
2. The company provides training to assist the "middles" in assuming a coaching/teaching role.	1	2	3	4	5
3. We have abandoned "direct-and-control" management in favor of more employee involvement.	1	2	3	4	5
4. Middle managers are encouraged to be entrepreneurs with responsibility for profit centers.	1	2	3	4	5
5. Our department heads and supervisors actively seek the opinion of line staff on ways of improving work processes.	1	2	3	4	5

Total points =

Summary Score

Record your total score for each section in the space below.

1. Knowledge of business   _____
2. Free flow of activity   _____
3. A stake in the company   _____
4. Positioned in the marketplace   _____
5. Managers who can lead   _____
6. Commitment from the "middles"   _____

Interpreting the Scores

The raw scores indicate the areas that offer the best opportunity for promoting resiliency and developing responsiveness in your organization. For a professional analysis, fax or mail the completed questionnaires to Deevy Gilligan International with the Response Form provided on the following page.

RESPONSE FORM

CREATING THE RESILIENT ORGANIZATION

We at Deevy Gilligan International have collaborated with people in organizations around the world during the past decade in applying and refining the concept of RapidResponse management. Whatever your organizational role, we are offering three major ways to support you in translating what you have read in Creating the Resilient Organization into practical value-adding applications in your organization. Use this Response Form to get additional information or to share your comments.

Applying RapidResponse Management

A one-day overview for executives, managers, labor leaders, and consultants interested in learning more about how to apply these concepts.

Identifying the Resilient Employee

We provide support in the use of the *Style Analysis* as a tool for assessing employee readiness for change.

Developing RapidResponse Consulting Skills

An intensive training course for internal and external consultants. Training is supported by *The RapidResponse Implementation Guide* (also available separately).

DEEVY GILLIGAN INTERNATIONAL

Please send me more information about:
__ Applying RapidResponse Management
__ Identifying Resilient Employees
__ Developing RapidResponse Consulting Skills
__ Complimentary *Style Analysis*
__ Please send me an analysis of my Readiness Checklist questionnaires

Name_____Title_____

Organization_____

Address_____City_____State_____Zip_____

Phone # (   ) _____ Fax # (   ) _____

Fax this form to: or   **Mail to:**   or   **Call:**
508-975-7691   Deevy Gilligan International   508-688-4900
                        203 Turnpike Street, Suite 404
                        North Andover, MA 01845

ABOUT THE AUTHOR

Edward Deevy is an internationally respected authority on transforming mature organizations into high-performance work environments. The defining element of Ed's work, expressed in all his writings, is a deeply held set of beliefs about the role of the individual employee.

Ed received his doctorate from the University of Massachusetts at Amherst where he has taught courses in management and organizational behavior. He is cofounder of Deevy Gilligan International (DGI), a research and development firm dedicated to the study of techniques and strategies required for introducing high-performance principles into mature work organizations. Headquartered in North Andover, Massachusetts, since 1985, DGI has supported the introduction of change in business and industrial corporations, public and private institutions, and school systems throughout North America and in Europe.

Ed's unique insights into the inner workings of corporations and institutions is derived from a background that combines study and research with over 15 years of in-the-trenches management experience. His international recognition as an authority on the human dimensions on change generates a continual demand for his speeches, training seminars, and presentations to various management development forums.

A native of Ireland, Ed became a naturalized U. S. citizen in 1967.

INDEX

Q

R

Z

DATE DUE

BRODART, CO.   Cat. No. 23-221-003